THE AWAKENED HEART PATH

SPIRITUAL TRANSFORMATION, ENLIGHTENMENT AND LOVE

KEVIN HUNTER

The Awakened Heart Path

ISBN 978-0-9829719-0-1

For more info, resources and assistance please go to www.Awakened-Heart-Path.com

ACKNOWLEDGMENTS

This book is the result of the effort of several people to whom I am grateful, for their love and contribution. The first is Susan George who did a wonderful job of editing. I am indebted to her for her love, support, friendship and assistance over many years.

Next, I would like to thank Lira Bennet, Gretchen Ross, and Nora Morris for their participation in the Awakened Heart Path from its inception and for their ongoing support over many months of videotaping and transcribing my talks which were used to create this book.

I am also grateful to Alan Lowenshuss and Angeliea Carson for inviting people to the Awakened Heart meditation group as well as for their personal friendship over the past several years.

It is from these meditation groups and the sessions given over the past year, that the Awakened Heart Path finally grew wings.

A heartfelt thanks all souls past and present who have blazed a spiritual path of the Heart. We are now at a special time on the planet, for the Spiritual Heart is reaching another stage of Awakening.

FOREWORD

"The beauties of the highest heavens and the marvels of the most sublime realms are all within the Heart: this is where the perfectly open and aware spirit concentrates."

The Secret of the Golden Flower

I encourage you to read this book as a meditation, contemplation and consideration of the human spiritual journey.

Allow yourself to approach the words, ideas and concepts shared in these pages, from a deep silent space within your Heart. Read the words, feel the energy behind the words and allow yourself to be receptive.

These words were written from an Aware, Heart-Felt, and Conscious Space. By being open and present from your own Heart as you read, you will align yourself with the intention of this book which is to facilitate your greater Spiritual Awakening.

If it is your time to Awaken and or deepen spiritually, you will feel a natural alignment, resonance and understanding on an energetic level with what is being shared.

For those who feel a resonance with this message just know that there are other Souls who are similarly awakening to the deeper dimensions of the Spiritual Heart at this time on the planet.

For truly the Heart is the seat of the Soul and the eternal doorway to balanced spiritual growth, transformation and human fulfillment in this lifetime. From my Heart to your Heart...... Blessings

CONTENTS

APPENDICIES

CHAPTER ONE

The Awakened Heart Path...
Unfolding your Divine Human Potential

Let's begin the exploration of the Awakened Heart Path (abbreviated A.H.P.). This path has been developed from more than 25 years of personal experience, study, practice and research into holistic, spiritual transformation.

The A.H.P. is based on eternal spiritual wisdom that can assist one to connect to that which is infinite, unconditional and eternal.

This is available to all who choose to look within the spiritual depths of their own Heart.

It is only when one connects to the depths of the subtle Spiritual Heart that they can discover and live from a place of love, truth, joy and freedom.

From the depths of an Awakened Heart arises the Self-Awareness of one's true nature as eternal Consciousness that is forever free, happy and unlimited.

All human beings have an impulse to grow, evolve and transform and that impulse originates from the depths of each person's Heart.

It is this doorway of the Heart that connects one's seemingly separate body and mind with the greater Infinite Reality.

Therefore, the way to rediscover who you truly are as an eternal Conscious Being is by reconnecting with the deeper dimensions of your Heart. I refer to this as The Awakened Heart.

Most people live their life in an unaware state, very similar to sleep, in regards to who they are as a Spiritual Being. Who you are spiritually transcends life, death and all self-limiting identities.

This state of deep unaware sleep does not allow an individual to experience the joy of existence that comes from within.

Inherent in each person's soul is an unending source of joy, love and happiness which is beyond compare to normal mundane worldly experiences.

Our true spiritual nature is totally unconditional and infinite as is the Universe that we all live in.

This radical bliss and inner spiritual freedom is something that most human beings will never experience. It exists only as an untapped, unawakened, hidden potential.

The majority of human beings experience their separateness, their isolation and their inability to connect with a deeper, more unified Reality.

Thus from the beginning of time, mankind has been driven to find answers to the meaning and purpose of life.

Ultimately, this evolved into the formation and creation of spiritual systems and teachings as well as organized religions.

There are many spiritual paths and methods to assist and guide one's human life towards greater spiritual awakening. However, unless that path involves the Heart at a core level, it will not be sufficient to bring forth the answers that lie deep within each person's soul.

For these answers to come, each human being must evolve holistically in Body, Mind and Heart-Spirit to reach their full potential. Then the Truth will become self-evident through direct inner Awareness and Experience.

The way we begin life in the womb and how we develop, is really quite interesting.

Science confirms that the first thing that happens a few days after conception is the formation, then the beating of the Heart.

The Heart is driving and sustaining our personal growth and development right from the very beginning of life.

During the development of the physical body from childhood into adulthood, the individual soul loses connection with its true spiritual nature and therefore with Reality as it truly is.

Simultaneous to this is the withdrawal of sensitivity, feeling and awareness of the Heart itself.

The core awareness of who you are as a spiritual being is lost in this process of growth and development into a separate individual with a personal ego identity.

Instead of being aware that you are eternal spiritual awareness and presence you become reduced to being identified with a physical body and with a personal ego that is confined within time and space.

The Awakened Heart Path is a holistic spiritual system that is designed to assist in reconnecting you with your original spiritual nature as Presence and Awareness.

In order to fulfill this Heartfelt spiritual intention each individual must undertake an inner journey of transformation at the levels of Body, Mind and Heart-Spirit.

For the most part these different aspects are disconnected and undeveloped within each human being. This causes the experience and awareness of unity and wholeness to be lost.

Therefore, rather than living life in the experience of fragmentation and separation, which is limitation, you can begin the process of harmonizing and developing these primary dimensions of human experience (emotional, mental and physical).

The Awakened Heart Path is a path of great return and a path of evolution. This is talked about in various spiritual traditions.

It refers to the fact that the human spiritual journey is a process of returning to one's true Spiritual Essence.

Returning to one's Essence allows one to stay in touch with Reality as it really is rather than as interpreted through one's personal ego filters.

These filters color and reduce Reality to being nothing but a poor reflection of its true self.

Consider the words, "in touch", which means to have the ability to connect to and to feel what, actually is. It is about being connected.

In this case what is being talked about is the ability to palpably discover, touch and feel that which you are, as Consciousness.

Thus, the path of great return is about being in touch with who you are as a spiritual being while living, breathing and experiencing life through a human body.

Once you are in touch with your spiritual essence, with Consciousness, then your spiritual journey can effectively unfold.

The only way that this can realistically be accomplished is if the individual begins the process of uncovering the deeper spiritual aspects and qualities of the Heart.

The Heart acts as an authentic compass to one's journey of human and spiritual transformation.

The Awakened Heart is also the rarest treasure that one could ever hope to find or discover.

Many spiritual traditions share the understanding that the greatest treasure is not a material thing, a worldly state of experience, or another lifetime that you might have in the future.

The Divine treasure is the essential reality that exists within the deepest levels of each person's Heart right here and right now.

Unfortunately, few human beings ever awaken to this treasure buried deep within their chest. Yet, in fact it is the only thing that has any lasting value and significance.

A quote from one saint says "That which has the greatest value is invisible to the eye."

Therefore that which you are seeking in life is not something that you will be able to see with your physical eyes or to acquire as a material thing.

You will have to discover it with your inner awareness through inner exploration coupled with the intention to unfold your spiritual potential.

The only balanced way to do this is by being in touch with the spiritual dimensions of the Heart.

Pause from reading and notice what is happening in your Heart in this very moment. What do you feel and sense there?

This is what is of value. This is what you want to learn to attune your inner awareness to.

It is important to progressively learn to be in touch with this, moment by moment, inner experience of the Heart. The deeper spiritual essence of the Heart is always present if you are present to it.

When you are in touch with the essence of the Heart you will experience it as an energy that has a spatial, warm sensation of Loving Presence.

The love and happiness that all human beings seek in life comes from the awakening, progressive opening and transformation of the Heart.

The Spiritual Heart has three primary aspects that can be developed over time. These can simply be referred to as depth, height and width.

As your inner awareness expands, grows and unfolds, you are awakening to depth within the Heart. This is an ever deepening inner experience and transformation of your spiritual awareness.

When you progress deeper into Presence, you are journeying into the depths of the Heart through feeling and awareness.

Most people never explore the inner depths of their Spiritual Heart.

It is very similar to traveling the world on a beautiful ocean liner and never getting off the boat to dive beneath the surface and discover what exists there.

This is how most human beings live their entire life, which is on the surface of existence; unaware of the riches that lie in the depths of their Being.

A common mistake that many people make is to assume that what they are currently aware of and what they are experiencing in their day to day life is Reality.

Yet, all normal human experience relates to the surface of the Heart, not to its depths. Thus life becomes a repetition of the same thing day in and day out with nothing real and profound taking place.

It is only when you begin to dive beneath the surface level of existence that you discover your inner depths of "Being".

The portal for this discovery is the Heart. It is only by progressively peeling back the layers of limitation, contraction and stress within the Heart that it becomes possible to experience true lasting happiness and peace.

Most people experience a feeling of separation, moment by moment, from other people, things and events in their life. This is a direct indication of being disconnected from the depths of the Heart.

The deeper you journey into your Heart the more connected you will feel within yourself, with the people around you and ultimately to the Infinite Unconditioned Reality of eternal existence.

The next dimension has to do with the width of the Heart. This relates to how much your Heart can encompass and it is an important factor in determining the quality of your relationships.

Let's look into the word communicate; the root of this word is "commune". However, the "commune" portion of the word has largely been lost these days in people's personal interactions with one another.

Now days it is mostly communication without any communion or personal connection taking place.

This has been accentuated recently by technology as we mostly relate to each other via computers, cell phones and or texting.

Width or breadth has to do with your ability to embrace and commune with your fellow human beings.

It is to embrace them with love, equality and the direct inner awareness that at the core of each individual lies the same love and Consciousness that resides within yourself.

This energy and inner awareness flows freely from an open Heart and a non-judgmental mind that is focused, centered and grounded in the present moment.

If your Heart is closed people will only hear your words but will not feel your Heart Energy that lies beneath the words. It is only a wide open Heart that allows for real communion to occur which leads to the experience of unity and oneness with all beings.

The final primary aspect of the Heart is height. Height relates to spiritual ecstasy, bliss and joy that transcends the seeming separateness of life in a human body.

This dimension of height, which is focused on in many spiritual traditions has to do with what has traditionally been called "Enlightenment".

The height of your Heart is the vertical dimension that culminates in the experience of divine light and the transcendence of a separate personal sense of self, by merging with the Universal or Divine Self.

A common error in many spiritual systems these days is the attempt to become Enlightened without developing holistic balance in Body, Mind and Heart-Spirit.

There are many teaching's these days that focus on Ascension or transcendence at the expense of worldly human existence.

You have to be extremely grounded in order to remain stable in these vertical experiences of transcendence and bliss. Being grounded is also essential to being integrated and whole.

That is why The Awakened Heart Path brings into consideration and exploration what I call the "Pillars of Life Harmony".

The Pillars of Life Harmony are:

- relationships
- work
- environment
- physical health
- emotional healing and growth

Ultimately, the Heart has to do with love which is an expression of harmony and balance. In order for the Heart to keep growing it needs to be supported by a harmonious life.

Therefore it is the responsibility of each individual to consciously cultivate harmony in all areas of their life, especially those outlined in the Pillars of Life Harmony.

Whatever you have experienced in your past, if it has created an imprint of stress and disharmony within you then it will limit your spiritual growth.

Unless you have had the great fortune to grow up in an enlightening, loving family, these obstructions are going to be there. These inner blockages are quite normal for the vast majority of mankind.

Unfolding your Divine Human Potential

In the greater awakening of the Heart it is important to explore your mental programs and conditioning that are self-limiting in relation to your greater spiritual transformation.

It is important to become aware of any belief patterns that are negative. These programs are self-destructive.

All negativity is stress and stress creates a contraction in your energy field and therefore your spiritual awareness.

This stress impacts the Heart which limits the flow of inner love and joy. As you progress on your path, all these aspects need to be looked at, harmonized and transformed.

The Awakened Heart Path is a holistic approach that addresses these various aspects that relate to the evolution and transformation of the Heart. This is important because the Heart is the doorway to your True Spiritual Nature.

It is important before you begin and or continue your inner spiritual Heart journey that you clearly decide that you really want to transform and awaken.

Apart from a rare few, the rest of us have to put in the work, time and energy that is required to unravel the obstructions and patterns that keep us from being fully present, aware and happy.

Therefore, it is important to ask yourself are you are serious about unfolding and growing your Spiritual Heart?

Are you willing to go through the transformation that is required? Do you have dedication, passion, focus and commitment to the spiritual path?

The good news is that even if you are weak in these attributes they can be developed.

It only takes your intention and willingness to begin this inner and outer journey of spiritual transformation. This is what the Awakened Heart Path is about.

It is about individuals who have an intention to cultivate and awaken their true spiritual nature and human potential.

It is about providing the support, wisdom and guidance that makes this process smoother, more efficient, effective and direct.

I am always inspired by any individual who demonstrates a real desire to unfold their Divine Human Potential through the Awakened Heart.

CHAPTER TWO

Sunrise of the Deep Heart -
The Next Stage of Humanity's Spiritual Evolution

To understand the next stage of humanity's spiritual evolution and how it relates to the Awakening of the Heart, we have to look at the history of our race over the past two thousand years.

Specifically, we need to focus on those cultures who have spoken of the importance of the current time-period we live in.

Some of the best-known and publicized information that has come out in the last ten to twenty years is from the Mayan civilization. The Mayans are particularly famous for their accuracy in predicting time.

They developed an ability to read the stars and to tap into the natural rhythms not only of the earth, and our solar system, but also of our entire galaxy.

As they explored their understanding of these natural rhythms, the Mayans concluded that changes in our solar system and galaxy create significant changes for life on earth.

The largest time-period they explored was the 26,000-year galactic cycle, a cycle that looks at our entire galaxy. The Mayans discovered that within this cycle, a unique event occurs at the midpoint of each cycle.

Every 13,000 years, our solar system lines up with what they called the "central sun" which lies at the center of our galactic system.

As our planet and solar system come into alignment with the central galaxy, we begin to receive energy and radiance from the central sun.

This has a great impact on life here on planet earth. Once again, we are in this revolutionary time-period.

Our sun gives us warmth and energy when it rises and invites us to enter our sleep cycle, when it sets. For the past 12,000 years, humanity has been in a spiritual sleep cycle.

Although evolution and transformation have occurred throughout this timespan, most of humanity has been asleep to the more subtle, awakened states of Consciousness.

In short, humanity has been asleep to its greater spiritual potential.

We are now going into a period of alignment with the central sun. Many people talk about 2012 as being the date of this alignment. However, it is not just the year 2012; it is really the time-period we are currently in.

Therefore, the next few years, along with 2012 and beyond are about humankind experiencing a spiritual awakening. That awakening is progressively taking place right now.

With any change and transformation, there is chaos and upheaval.

You can see from the tsunami several years ago to the more recent earthquakes in Chile and Haiti that there are catastrophic events taking place on the planet.

All of these changes have been predicted and prophesized.

As we move from a state of being asleep, to awakening there will be ongoing periods of upheaval, chaos, destruction, and basic unrest all over the planet.

All of this is necessary. In order for humanity to break out of the mold it has been in, there has to be a process of breaking apart the old rigid structures.

This can be seen clearly in the U.S.A, where the U.S. government and the economy are going through a major transition and transformation.

Many of the old models and paradigms that humanity has functioned within have to be reconfigured and restructured.

This is essential so that the higher Consciousness, which is at the root of all of existence, has the opportunity to take hold within our society.

It is only when these rigid structures start to shift throughout human society, that Consciousness can begin the greater awakening of humanity on a global scale.

When this occurs, the people who have been asleep to their greater spiritual potential will gradually begin to wake up.

This is a radical change from what has been happening on the planet for the last several thousand years.

Certainly, there have always been spiritual systems and practitioners living consciously focused lives in small groups and communities across the planet.

However they made up an extremely small percentage of the population, perhaps 1,000-5,000 people per million.

The waking up process happening at this time is about many people experiencing a breakthrough in their awareness.

This awakening will allow deeper states of consciousness and spiritual awareness to emerge on a much larger scale.

This new awakening is not arising as religious ideology. Most religions are not about authentic Awakening. They are simply a set of spiritual beliefs that rarely lead to a permanent state of Enlightenment.

The emergence of this new structure and paradigm is ideally facilitated by the conscious participation of each individual.

Change is going to happen, change is coming, and one of the great things about being alive in the human body and being here on this planet is that we have a choice to participate in the change.

At this time, each individual has a choice to either wake up and consciously participate in the next stage of humanity's spiritual evolution or by default, be dragged along by the process of change.

Choosing the latter will of course make the transitional experience much more difficult.

The inner chaos, emotional and mental upheaval and discomfort will be greatest for those who do not understand what this time is about and how to participate consciously.

Those who are asleep will be unaware that there is even a choice to begin with, let alone be aware that they can consciously choose to align with the transformation that is unfolding.

This alignment is what I refer to as "The Sunrise of the Deep Heart" or the alignment of the collective Heart of humanity with its true spiritual purpose.

The ever-increasing life force energy that is the result of our progressive alignment with the central sun will drive this change deep from within each human being. This subtle life force energy is already affecting us.

It is not like the energy of our sun, which you feel as heat on your body. This life force is working on a very subtle emotional and psychological level of people's Consciousness.

It works on the subconscious and unconscious dimensions to bring about deep transformation.

Therefore, "The Sunrise of the Deep Heart" is the awakening of each individual to his or her greater spiritual potential and evolution. It is up to each person to choose to participate consciously in this next stage of transformation.

As you "awaken", you become conscious of the dimension I refer to as the Awakened Heart. This is the center of our spiritual reality and the doorway to greater spiritual unfolding.

This process of awakening and spiritual transformation is what I refer to as "The Awakened Heart Path".

The Awakened Heart Path assists an individual to align consciously with the inner transformation that is happening at this time.

Individuals can best assist themselves to align with the coming changes by taking up an ongoing daily practice that involves working with the energy within their own Heart.

This is a process of deeply connecting with your Heart and the subtle spiritual energy contained within it.

It is about feeling the vibration in your Heart, feeling the energies that are there, and seeing what insights and information arise.

Another important aspect of the Awakened Heart practice is consciously establishing an energetic Heart connection and resonance with other people and with mother earth, Gaia.

It is also about connecting via your Heart to the spiritual dimension of consciousness as awareness, presence and unconditional love.

The Sunrise of The Deep Heart is a transformational process that continuously unfolds. Your human life is always unfolding, developing, transforming and growing.

As you become more and more conscious of your Spiritual Heart, you may directly experience a palpable, vibrational energy there.

This is what you are attempting to get in touch with as you begin your practice of feeling your Heart energy and its awareness. The Heart area literally starts to vibrate.

It starts to vibrate in a way that will progressively allow you to Wake Up. When this Heart Presence becomes conscious, focused and stable over time, then one becomes the Awakened Heart.

This living vibration of the Heart opens the doorway to a greater spiritual reality that is the very essence of everyone and everything.

From that point on it is this spiritual vibration, which directly and efficiently helps an individual to unfold their human spiritual life with divine balance and in harmony with the whole.

Life then is no longer a belief driven process but an Awareness driven process, free from the restrictive limitations of the mind and its incessant criticism and judgment of each arising moment.

Thus, the way to best facilitate your spiritual transformation is by aligning your intention to awaken with the inner power of the Heart.

CHAPTER THREE

Spiritual Flowering...The Point of Human Existence

Life is about unfolding our true self and our true potential. This entails the complex task of developing inner spiritual awareness while at the same time, balancing our outer human life.

Spiritual flowering is a process of opening to beauty.

So much beauty exists on the outside. You can watch a beautiful sunset, sit in nature by a lake or in the mountains or simply feel the beauty of being with someone you love.

As beautiful as all this is, the greatest beauty exists within you.

Unfolding your inner beauty is really the point of existence.

Cultivating inner beauty is what progressively leads one to experience a life that is fulfilling, joyful and full of love. This flowering involves an ever-greater expansion of inner awareness and spiritual presence.

Much of the time our awareness is absorbed in daily life and all the activities we find ourselves engaged in. All that activity and busyness tends to obscure inner beauty.

In order for inner beauty to have an opportunity to shine through and to be experienced, you have to deepen your connection to Spiritual Presence by being profoundly aware, in this present moment.

So much of our life is oriented towards what has happened in past moments or what is going to happen in future moments rather than on what is happening in the present moment.

It is only by directing your intention and focus inwards, that you can begin to access the inner dimension of beauty and presence and bring that into each moment of your life.

This is an inner unfolding and an inner process.

It is important to live your outer life with balance and to appreciate the beauty that exists in the world. It is equally if not more important for your spiritual unfolding, to seek the inner beauty of the spiritual dimension within yourself.

As you start to tap into that inner beauty, you will begin unfolding spiritual dimensions that are infinite in their scope and possibility.

These inner dimensions of beauty include many different experiences and facets of Consciousness. One of these is loving presence. This is very similar to the love a child feels from its mother's embrace.

Another is infinite peace and stillness that is free from effort and stress. This peace is always present within us, but it requires an active inner focus and inner awareness to consciously connect to it.

In addition to infinite peace, there is Universal Love. This love is unconditional. It does not depend on any relationship or action you perform.

Spiritual Flowering...The Point of Human Existence

It is not dependent upon you being a "good person" as determined by society's moral codes or by any of the conditioned mental belief systems you have developed over a lifetime.

This love is accessible only through your Heart and its deeper dimensions, which unfold and flower over time.

This is the unfolding of inner spiritual beauty. As your Heart opens and awakens to truth or reality, it progressively unfolds petal by petal and the beauty that exists within you begins to shine forth and radiate.

Another fundamental quality of who you are as a spiritual being is infinite radiance. This infinite light illuminates and radiates your entire form.

It "lives" your physical body, powers your mind, and gives you the emotional qualities and experiences that you have in life. This infinite radiant life force is the fundamental building block of your existence as a human being.

Spiritual flowering is something that unfolds gradually. It is important to understand that this is a progressive process.

You can look at this process as being comprised of four phases or stages within each person's development.

The first stage begins when a person is in the womb and goes through the process of being born. This stage continues for the first year or two of life and is known as the pre-personal stage.

The pre-personal stage is the period before your identity and sense of self, your "I-sense" and all the concepts, images, beliefs and structures that go with that, have been formed.

At the pre-personal stage there is no distinction between what is inside you and what is outside. It is all one in the infant's experience, yet the conscious Awareness and Recognition that it is all One, has not yet developed.

The 2nd stage begins the creation that ultimately ends up as your personal sense of self or "I", also referred to as the "persona" and the "ego". This develops from early childhood and continues until one's late teenage years.

This is your ego identity and you carry it throughout your entire life, unless you awaken.

Consider the following analogy of the sunrise in relation to the stage two development of the "I" self.

Before the sunrise everything is pitch black, there is no ability to observe or know the surrounding environment as long as there is darkness.

Then the sun begins to rise and the increase in light gradually reveals the forms and shapes of the surrounding landscape.

In our early years what is revealed by the inner light is our ego self, which gradually coalesces into the shape of our individual identity – our sense of "I".

This inner "I" then becomes our reference point from the moment we wake up until the time we go to sleep, every single day of our life.

The core of this second stage development is the personal self. It is the sense of existing as an independent being that is distinct and separate from other human beings and from the world around it.

Spiritual Flowering...The Point of Human Existence

The personal self is the inner reference point and the sense of "who I am" moment to moment.

It is characterized by the word "I": I am feeling.... I have to do.... I need to get ready for work now and so on.

Once this "I-sense" or ego forms, it becomes the primary foundation from which most people live and experience their life. Every event whether judged to be good or bad by the mind, is seen from the point of view of the ego self.

It is very rare that a person spontaneously transcends the second stage personal "I-sense" and moves onto the third stage of human development.

However, as an individual continues to unfold in their life, they may progressively open into this third stage, known as the transpersonal stage.

The third, transpersonal stage of development has to do with the foundation of who you are as spiritual consciousness.

It is about the part of you that existed prior to this life and will continue to exist after this life is over.

The transpersonal dimension transcends your personal life, your human body, and all the personal experiences you have in this lifetime.

The primary aim and focus of many spiritual systems and paths is to awaken to the transpersonal dimension. As you become aware of this dimension your entire inner experience changes.

It awakens an aspect that remains hidden and dormant in the vast majority of people on the planet.

The Sufis have a saying that "Each human being's True Essence is like a hidden treasure".

This hidden treasure reveals itself during the transpersonal stage of development.

It is only when an individual begins to wake up to the spiritual qualities of universal awareness, presence, light and subtle energy that they start to activate the transpersonal dimension.

This is the final goal of many spiritual traditions but there is another possible stage of development that lies beyond it.

The fourth stage of human spiritual development has to do with the integration of the transcendental spiritual dimension with the second stage, personal identity.

This leads to what I call Integrated Enlightenment of the Human dimension with the Spiritual dimension.

To unfold the fourth stage of development requires the harmonization and alignment of the physical body, the emotional body and the mental body.

It is a process.

This is where the importance of the Heart enters into the spiritual process.

Without the Heart and the awakening of the subtler dimensions of the spiritual Heart center, it is not possible to integrate the personal and transpersonal.

Many spiritual paths specifically cultivate and focus on the transpersonal third stage. This can ultimately be very dangerous because the individual has not fully journeyed the other stages.

Therefore the person is not yet whole and balanced on all levels, which can lead to delusion in regards to their spiritual state and experience.

This in turn can create a negative ripple effect on all those around them. It is of the utmost importance to be fully integrated and aligned with the loving presence of the Awakened Heart.

It is quite common to see spiritual teachers, priests, monks and so on who have great difficulty in integrating their physical, psychological, emotional and sexual energies with the higher more refined spiritual energies, of the third stage of experience.

This is due to the fact that they have not done the work to integrate the third stage transpersonal with the second stage ego personality or simply put: body, mind and feelings.

Most human beings remain stuck at the personal stage of development and never fully awaken the inner dimensions of who they are as a spiritual being.

It is also possible to become stuck within these various levels of development which again causes stagnation and blocks further integration and wholeness.

Therefore, if you want to complete your destiny, if you want to know who you are as a spiritual being so that you can spiritually flower, you must involve the Heart in the spiritual path that you find yourself on.

The Heart helps us to develop in a compassionate, balanced way.

This requires opening to the subtler energy dimensions of the Heart. It also means bringing the qualities of feeling, awareness, and sensitivity into each moment of your life.

As you unfold your spiritual journey the Heart will provide many insights into the all the different aspects of yourself that are not in harmony.

It will bring to the light of awareness to those parts of you that need further refinement in order for the fourth stage integration to take place.

The fourth stage of development continues throughout the entirety of one's life.

There is no end to the unfolding, development and integration of ever higher states of Love, Peace and Presence.

The cosmos has been unfolding for 15 billion years and will continue to do so for billions of years into the future. Likewise, our soul is infinite and eternal and will continue this unfolding and flowering over eons of time.

The whole point of the Divine, of Consciousness, of Reality, God - however you like to refer to it - is to unfold this intention to wake up and be fully conscious and aware as an integrated-human-spiritual-being.

This impulse to grow, transform and evolve is fundamental to the nature of Consciousness.

The flow of Consciousness is always moving towards the integration of what is transcendental with what is imminent.

Spiritual Flowering...The Point of Human Existence

This is the impulse to bring the qualities of the transpersonal and personal into the present moment in an integrated fashion.

This can only happen through the activation and awakening of your Heart.

I am referring here, to the spiritual aspect of your Heart which is aware of even the subtlest vibrations and energies.

Through insight, intelligence, contemplation, and consideration you make choices in your life that either assist in unfolding the process of spiritual flowering, or become an impediment to it.

Each Soul is on a personal journey to learn that which will lead them to greater wholeness and oneness, whether it takes one or many lifetimes.

Through a process of discovery and experience you will eventually learn the lessons of life which have to do with alignment to the eternal principles of love and harmony.

You will learn through trial and error that anything you do that is focused solely on the personal self the ego I, is never sufficient to create lasting happiness and peace within yourself.

This is the reason to awaken beyond your personal sense of self to your transpersonal self and then to ultimately integrate the personal and transpersonal dimensions.

As you begin this process, the spiritual flowering of your soul will shine through and awaken aspects of your being that are currently dormant and deeply asleep.

These are the deeper stages of human development. Only an exceptionally small percentage of people out of the billions on our planet will wake up and fully embrace this most radical of human possibilities.

The point of human existence is to discover that life and Consciousness, the very Essence of who you are, is eternal.

By discovering and awakening to this eternal Truth of existence, your Soul will be set free to enjoy the Infinite Beauty of Oneness, Love and Harmony.

CHAPTER FOUR

The Keys to Inner Happiness

Every human being is constantly seeking happiness.

Everything an individual does is ultimately being motivated by or is tied to, an impulse deep within their soul to be happy. It resides at the very core of each of us.

Just as the heart beats and pulses in each moment, so too does universal Consciousness.

This pulse is experienced by man, as an impulse to unfold into ever-greater states of Happiness.

The degree to which you experience authentic Happiness is a direct indicator of how closely you are aligned and resonant with, this impulse of Consciousness.

To further describe this impulse for Happiness, here is a beautiful story from the Sufi tradition.

"Once upon a time, before the universe was created, God or Consciousness was considering manifesting the universe and creating human beings.

As God considered the human race, he asked himself "Where should I hide the key to human happiness?"

He pondered this for eons of time. First, he considered hiding the key in the depths of the ocean.

Then God realized that human beings would eventually have the intelligence to create a submarine which would enable them to go to the depths of the ocean.

So God decided that would be far too easy. After further contemplation, he considered putting it on the moon. Of course, in his brilliance and foresight, he saw that humankind would eventually go to the moon.

Then after much contemplation and consideration the light bulb went off.

God decided to hide the key to human happiness within each person's Heart; because that is the last place they will ever look".

This story really summarizes and personifies the human spiritual journey.

In the search for happiness, human beings look in so many different places and directions. Rarely do they stop long enough to bring a greater awareness and focus to the Heart that beats within their very own chest.

When you look at the human journey and how we live our lives, it is very similar to a miner finding Fools Gold.

In the past when miners panned for gold, they often came across a substance that was shiny, metallic, and yellowish and almost identical to real gold. This metal became known as Fools Gold.

When human beings seek happiness outside themselves in their relationships, their jobs, or even through activities that benefit others, they only find Fools Gold - temporary moments of joy that look and feel like the real experience.

Unfortunately, these experiences never lead to the discovery of the "real gold" which is a permanent state of Happiness that arises from the depths of one's very own Heart.

If an individual is constantly engaged in a lifestyle that does not allow any time to be still, centered and aware beyond the surface level of existence, there is no opportunity to discover their real "Heart of Gold".

A very interesting experience happens when we turn our attention and energy to mining the gold within our own Heart.

As you become more centered and grounded in the present moment, a palpable, energetic vibration and presence can be directly felt, deep within the chest.

Many traditions talk about the seat of the soul, by this they mean the gateway to universal Consciousness or universal Presence and this is understood to reside within the Heart.

Therefore, in order for you to reconnect with that essential foundation deep within your being, you have to bring focused awareness and intention to this journey of inner discovery.

For the most part people's awareness is stuck on a superficial level.

This is because they are caught up moment by moment, in the activities and sensations of the physical body, their thinking, their mind processes and the senses in general.

Whatever they are seeing, hearing or saying, absorbs their attention. Even tactile sensations in the body or odors can become a focus of attention.

Unless you consciously choose to focus your attention and awareness within the Heart area, you will not experience these deeper aspects of your Spiritual-Self.

This is because your attention and therefore your energy, is too fragmented. A laser like focus is required to penetrate the deeper layers of who you are, beyond the mundane levels of human experience.

Your focus has to become like a laser beam that is concentrated through a magnifying lens.

I'm sure many of you in your childhood have taken a magnifying glass, focused the energy of the sun through the lens and watched the power of that focused energy actually burn or ignite something.

In a similar way when you focus with concentration, determination, and persistence you are becoming like a magnifying lens.

Then the energy of Consciousness that resides within you can begin to burn away the layers of obstruction, confusion, and the delusion of the false ego.

Once this occurs, you start to penetrate the deeper layers of the Heart and begin to connect with the universal life force energy. This energy then helps to peel away and remove the inner blockages.

The Keys to Inner Happiness

There is a lot of talk about the movement of energy in different spiritual traditions.

In the kundalini tradition the focus is on the movement of Kundalini energy from the base of the spine up to the crown of the head.

In other traditions such as the Taoist tradition, energy is consciously circulated around the body in a circular motion. This is called the Micro Cosmic Orbit.

There are many other energy centers or chakras and meridian systems cultivated in different spiritual traditions.

However, the original energy system, the foundation and origin of all energy in relation to the individual body-mind is located at the core of the Heart.

This core life current exists within every individual.

Unless you peel through the various stresses and obstructions within your Heart using a laser like focus, you will be unable to fully flow the life-force current and actualize a fully Awakened Heart within this lifetime.

Only by awakening and living through your Heart can you realize your ultimate human spiritual potential.

Do not become fascinated by spiritual energy and experiences especially if they take you away from the depth of your Heart. All these things are distractions to a greater awakening.

Therefore, it is important for each individual to keep in mind that the seat of the soul, that spark of Consciousness, resides in the Heart.

This divine spark illuminates, radiates, and lives the body-mind-emotional experience we each have, moment by moment.

Yet most people never recognize this because again their attention, their awareness is too fragmented by other activities, sensations and experiences of "humanness".

There is another quote that I like very much from Carl Jung. He says, "Your vision will become clear only when you look inside the Heart. Those who look outside the Heart just dream. Those that look inside awaken".

Let's examine that: "Your vision will become clear only when you look inside the Heart." This is really a summation of what I have been talking about.

Your experience of your true self will only be discovered when your vision is clear. Moreover, your vision can only be clear when you are looking into the depths of your Heart.

Everything else that arises is a modification of that original energy, such as our thoughts, feelings etc.

An easy way to understand this is using the example of pure white light: You can break white light down into a spectrum of colors. However, no matter how many different shades of colors there are, they still originate from the original beam of white light.

The whole spectrum of colors, everything that we see in our human experience is in a very real sense, a fragmentation of the original light and energy which is our spiritual essence.

All our experience, our thoughts, the feelings we have in our body, our day to day experiences, are just a fragmentation of that original energy, of that original life force current.

In order to experience the life force current directly, while awake, while present, you have to penetrate the deeper layers of the Heart.

To do that, you need to cultivate a regular practice of focusing into your Heart.

A good way to begin to unfold this understanding is by looking at the physical anatomy of the Heart itself. In humans, the heartbeat originates in a small group of cells called the Sino Atrial Node.

The Sino Atrial Node is the pacemaker of the Heart. It tells the Heart to beat and depending on the situation, this happens approximately once every second. More if a person is exercising or less if they are sleeping.

This small group of cells is fed by the primal life force current that we have been talking about. This current connects us to universal Presence, to universal Consciousness.

If you are going to focus into your Heart then you have to know exactly where to place your focus.

There is a very simple way to do this: Using the palm of your hand, take your hand and place the heel of your palm on the center of your chest.

Then place your pinkie finger over the nipple area and bring your thumb down so that all of your fingers are touching one another. About half way up your thumb, within a small radius is the Sino atrial node.

This area is the gateway to the original current of Consciousness before it becomes blocked and contracted by the process of ego identity.

If you are looking at the center of your chest, it is slightly to the left of center, about four fingers above the middle of the chest and within an area about the size of a quarter.

When meditating bring your attention to that area and let it be your primary focus. Feel deeply into that part of the Heart while maintaining an awareness of your overall physical body.

Concentrated focus on this region of the Heart will allow you to progressively awaken this primal energy.

Until you begin to connect with this source energy through the core of your Heart, your awareness and therefore your focus, will always be drawn to and absorbed by other functions of the body, mind and senses.

As Human beings, we develop in stages. When we are born we have no sense of our individuality, we have not yet formed our persona.

As we develop into early childhood, we begin to develop a sense of "I". That sense of "I" is a collection of all the images, feelings, and experiences we have ever had.

From early childhood, these aspects become solidified into what becomes the persona, which is taken to be reality, rather than for the conditioned experience that it really is.

The Keys to Inner Happiness

It is very rare that an individual gains the wisdom and insight that leads them to penetrate into the deeper dimensions of the Spiritual Heart.

That is why it is so important that a person consciously chooses and invites the greater awakening of their Heart.

Most people do not awaken to the experience of pure, unconditional love and presence because this dimension of themselves has receded from their conscious awareness.

They have become unconscious to it and are therefore unable to connect to this original gateway.

The challenge of walking the Awakened Heart Path is that you have to cultivate the depths of the Heart itself. This is a process that has to be consciously chosen.

Lack of connection to these deeper levels of the Heart is the main reason for the sense of separateness that most human beings experience in their day-to-day existence.

If you examine your experience moment to moment, you will notice there is always an underlying feeling of separateness.

You sense that you are separate from other people, from the room, from the furniture that you are sitting on; from the car you drive and so on.

This sense of separateness is a key indicator that the Heart is blocked and that the universal spirit, the life current of Consciousness in its original form, is not flowing.

As you progress in the awakening of your Heart, gradually these layers of stress and tension that surround the Heart will be healed and dissolved.

Then, instead of experiencing separation from other people, things and events, you progressively experience the underlying unity that exists prior to all these experiences. This is what the Awakened Heart Path is about.

The Awakened Heart Path is about opening this gateway to universal Presence and to the universal life force, through the Heart.

Once that gateway opens it encompasses the whole Heart. The energy travels up from the Heart and back into the brain core. Then it travels in a circle, known as the microcosmic orbit, flowing down the front of the body and rising up the back, to the top of the head.

The second part of its path from the base of the spine to the top of the head is referred to as the Kundalini energy.

You can do all kinds of practices, whether it is focusing on the Kundalini energy, following the Micro Cosmic Orbit, working with the chakras and so on, and still not connect with the original life current that resides within the Heart itself.

Really, the essence of spiritual enlightenment, of spiritual transformation, is to reconnect through your Heart with universal Consciousness and Presence.

You will know you have made this connection when there is a greater sense of unity with all life and a corresponding diminishing sense of separateness.

This has nothing to do with any other experiences you may have whether they are grand mystical experiences or mundane everyday human experiences. All of these are temporary.

The point of the spiritual journey and spiritual enlightenment is to discover that which eternal, not that which is temporary.

Experiences are not to be avoided or denied, but neither are they to be chased or held to be of any ultimate significance.

This is why the foundation of The Awakened Heart Path is to develop a greater sense of unity and Oneness and a greater sense of Loving Presence.

These are the primary indicators that show you how you are unfolding spiritually. Everything else is secondary and comes out of that underlying unity and Presence.

The reason why the journey is so difficult for most human beings is that their Heart is closed.

Because of this, they experience themselves as a separate being and have no underlying sense of oneness with the universe and people around them.

This feeling of separation leads to seeking for happiness but where do they seek?

Human beings seek through all kinds of avenues: Going out to a bar to drink alcohol, doing drugs, going to a variety of entertainments or seeking the perfect relationship to name a few.

Seeking happiness through mundane human experience is as much of an error as a monk living in a cave, who is seeking salvation through subtle mystical and spiritual experiences.

As long as you are searching anywhere for Happiness, other than in the depths of your own Heart, you are really wasting precious time.

The recognition of your eternal nature has to do with opening the depths of your Heart and consciously connecting to the eternal Presence that lies within yourself and within all of existence.

This is what is meant by being anchored in "Self-Awareness" – it is the awareness of your true and inherently Happy Self.

CHAPTER FIVE

Loving Presence...Opening the Heart to "Now"

"Are you present to the Now?"

Opening one's Heart to the "Now", is an extremely important part of the journey. Loving Presence is the very essence and foundation of who we are as spiritual beings and can only be known in the Now.

Human beings walk around in disguise, hidden under the layers of their personality-self which is the very thing that camouflages the truth of Loving Presence that is existing Now.

You are more than just this body and this lifetime. Loving Presence is the healing balm which will assist in bringing your soul back into a full connection with your Spiritual Essence, which is Consciousness itself.

This Loving Presence is what we are always seeking in our life, albeit unconsciously.

At the very foundation of our being, there is a deep desire and longing to fully "Be" and to embrace the life transforming power of Loving Presence. It is our very nature.

When you are not experiencing a connection with Love and Presence you will feel a sense of lack and emptiness, if you are at all aware and sensitive.

When love is not available to you in the present moment, you are divorced from reality and from the fundamental truth of who you are as Consciousness.

On a human level, being divorced from a life partner is always a distressful, uneasy, uncomfortable experience.

Likewise when we are disconnected from Loving Presence, these same feelings of being divorced and separate from Reality arise from the deepest part of our being.

The Heart (by this I am referring to more than just the physical heart) and the Loving Presence that lives through us, really are the most important and underutilized gifts that a person has.

However, the majority of people on planet are asleep to the aspect of reality known as "Loving Presence". This inner divorce creates a deep split within the body, mind and psyche of the unaware individual.

It is not until an individual begins to work with the energy of the Heart and opens to the Love that arises from within, that this deep inner split of body and mind can be healed.

When a person is divorced from their true essence, the fundamental feeling that arises is one of separateness.

There is a feeling of separateness not only from other people, but also from the experience of Oneness, Love and Harmony that is the very nature of reality.

This core feeling of separateness, whether conscious or unconscious, automatically drives a person to look for a solution.

If you are not happy, if you are not feeling love in this present moment, then you are driven to find love and to find a solution to your inner unrest and distress.

If you are aware and honest with yourself, you will feel that at your core, you are not yet totally Happy and Free.

Most people however, never do anything about this. There is just an unconscious agreement with our partners and with society at large that this is just the way things are.

When people are unhappy they always tend to look outside themselves rather than inside themselves for a real and lasting solution.

It becomes automatic to seek a solution to life's problems outside of ourselves. This is what is expected of each individual as conditioned by our society. Maybe if I make more money I will be happy, perhaps a better relationship will make me feel complete, and so forth.

If you are not experiencing union with truthful reality, you are not whole. You are not complete. In fact there is a deep hole within the very core of your being.

The experience of emptiness along with a sense of lack is an experience of blockage. This feeling will drive you to look for the solution through many different avenues of life such as being fulfilled by another person or in the form of spiritual practices.

However, once again this is the normal human pattern of looking outside in an attempt to complete the part of your being that feels something is missing.

The motivation to try to find something to heal and remove this experience of inner lack is an unconscious drive.

Until you go within and work with the healing unifying power of Loving Presence it will not be possible to experience continuous feelings of Love, Joy and Union.

This union is the experience of Universal Love. You may occasionally have glimpses of Universal Love, but it will dissolve again into the experience of separateness until the inner healing work is done.

As long as you are looking for something, you are separate from it.

Until you can relax sufficiently into the present moment, into Loving Presence, you will continue to search for it outside yourself in the form of another person or another experience.

As long as you are doing this, your soul cannot fully rest. This is the catch 22 of human existence.

A part of us knows we are not happy, knows our being is fragmented and broken. That awareness creates the pursuit for a sense of wholeness and completeness that seems to continuously evade our every attempt to capture it once and for all.

Most of us are never given a blueprint and a compass to successfully undertake this journey. Therefore, most of us fail in our quest for union, love and happiness.

We usually end up falling flat on our face, feeling frustrated and crushed by our failure and lack of success to transform our life experience.

Loving Presence...Opening the Heart to "Now"

To be successful in your life's quest to unify with Loving Presence, you will have to learn to navigate your way through the maze and challenge of human experience and existence. This is a day-to-day challenge.

It is important to ensure that your pursuits, activities, and even your spiritual practices do not engross you to the point that you obstruct and block this fundamental Presence from revealing itself to you.

What motivates YOU as a human being? Take a moment and look inside.

If you notice that your motivations are coming from a sense of incompleteness and emptiness, then look into your Heart and feel the energy that is there.

Look at what is happening in your Heart and see if you can discover what is perturbing you, what the conflict is and what the stress is.

Once you begin to work through the stress and inner conflicts within your being, your Heart will gradually open and grow to the next level. This allows you to be more present right Now.

"Now" does not exist in the past or in the future. Now is eternal and exists as a Presence that is fully alive and dynamic. This can be tapped into, felt and experienced in any moment that you are present.

Once you have established a deep connection with Loving Presence, there is no longer a sense of separateness from anyone or anything.

In our modern world, we have an incredible amount of information available to us via the internet regarding spiritual paths, religions, new age groups, different philosophical perspectives and all the various ideas that come out of these.

Thus for many people, Spirituality becomes more of a mental learning process than a clear and direct path about how to transform their life.

They may understand the meaning of what they read, and may think about being present, think about NOW and think about what it is to be Sourceful, awake, and free.

However, the actual experience of these things has nothing to do with thinking, or the mind. The whole point of connecting to Loving Presence within your Heart is to allow for the Experience and Awareness of Now, not the Concept of Now.

The concept of Now is not fulfilling. It is a temporary understanding, a fleeting experience that will vanish into the ethers just like all other life experiences.

When you truly connect to the doorway of Now through the Heart, you connect to that which is eternal and prior to manifestation, yet forms the very foundation and essence from which all life experience emerges.

From that point onwards, you will continue to be engaged in all the things that make up a normal human life; however you will engage life from a different place of awareness that is infused with the energy of Loving Presence.

Again, this does not arise from your mind or thoughts about Loving Presence. This has to occur tangibly and experientially through your Heart. It is not something that you can make up, imagine, or talk yourself into.

There is a lot of emphasis these days on positive thinking, New Age thinking etc. These ways of thinking have their place and usefulness.

Any method or modality has its place, but ultimately you have to go beyond the mental self-talk, even if it is positive talk and let it go.

Learn to be in the Presence of your own Heart.

As you explore that dimension of your Being, be aware of any inner positions you have, any posturing, attitudes and beliefs you are holding that make you rigid and inflexible.

The Heart does not know right or wrong, nor does it judge. The mind however, is different. In general, whenever the mind takes a position it carries a charge with it - take note of this very important point.

This is not to say that you cannot have preferences, but taking a position that has a charge to it, means you have identified yourself with that particular thought, belief or emotion.

The very act of identification puts a charge on a concept or belief, which creates distance and separation from the Loving Presence within. It keeps the door to Loving Presence closed.

For this reason, it is important to practice being present and to discover the attitudes and judgments that are creating tension and separation within your own Being.

Such patterns create tension in your Heart, which you feel as stress. This causes unhappiness and a lack of fulfillment.

When you lack fulfillment, you seek it outside yourself. Thus the cycle of feeling disconnected from the Loving Presence within, and seeking an outer solution to it, perpetuates itself ad infinitum.

Rather than tying your experience of happiness, love, and joy, to conditions, circumstances and people, practice connecting directly to Loving Presence in the moment. This is the Source of all Happiness.

Then gradually over time, you will experience the inner Love, Freedom and Peace that your Soul has searched lifetimes for.

Whatever arises in your day-to-day experience look into it, explore and examine it. If it is something that is causing stress, look and see what kind of mental or emotional position you are holding onto.

Ask; what am I doing in this moment that is not coming from Love?

Also what is not allowing Loving Presence to flow in this moment?

If you look at these issues, you will begin to heal and address the challenges you are facing that simply perpetuate unending suffering.

Loving Presence...Opening the Heart to "Now"

There are steps you can take to become open to the Now and to create an ongoing flow and transformation in your life. The first foundational step is to have the Intention to open your Heart to Loving Presence.

If you want to be open and if you want to love, you have to start with the intention to be that way. This is the first step.

An intention is more than just saying the words, "I want to be loving" it is a real desire to change and transform.

In relation to the exploration of Loving Presence, if you truly desire to experience it you would ask yourself "do I have the intention to love" right here in this present moment and in the next moment and the next and so on.

Most people do not have this intention to the degree that is required for real transformation. You must be willing to act on and engage this intention for transformation with real passion.

If you do not have the intention to love, how is your Heart going to open to the Now? Only you can choose Love. No one can or will ever be able to force you to open your Heart and Love. It is a personal choice.

Most likely you have filled your life up with many things and have engaged yourself in focuses that have nothing to do with the greater flowering of your Heart.

Therefore, you have to have the intention to be present and to love to begin the process of reorienting your life.

The second step is to have the courage to love.

For the most part people go through their lives lacking the inner courage to fully love.

Courage is important because it gives you the strength and determination to address the many challenges that will arise in the course of your human journey.

To be human is to be confronted with daily challenges. In addition there is the ongoing challenge of remaining in a state of harmony and balance despite the chaos that may be present in your personal life.

It takes courage to stand up and look at yourself; it takes courage to love. Most people are guarded and shut down when it comes to being loving and present.

People are afraid to love because of the fear of being hurt and disappointed the way they have been so many times in the past.

Therefore, many people think why make the effort to be love and to share love when there is the possibility of being disappointed once again.

Underlying all of this is the fear of rejection, the fear of being hurt. In order to move through this fear you need to find the courage within your own Heart.

It is tremendously helpful to be "Lion Hearted". This means to be strong, to be courageous. It is another fundamental quality of your Heart, if you choose to embrace it.

The third step is a commitment to love.

In addition to having the intention to love and the courage to love, you need the commitment to love which is really a commitment to your spiritual unfolding.

It has been said many times that love is the greatest healer. For the most part people do not make use of the healing power of Love.

People are so lost in their "busyness" that they are not even aware of their Heart, let alone the need to have the intention, commitment, and courage to love moment to moment.

To walk The Awakened Heart Path requires a deep commitment to love in each moment. Persistence is also necessary.

It is not about trying to love a few times here and there. It is through sheer determination and persistence to love that the Heart will open to Truth.

Ultimately, you are looking to change the non-loving ego based patterns and identities that keep your Heart imprisoned.

By patterns, I mean those things that make up your identity as an individual ego. It is this identity as a separate ego that separates you from experiencing the Loving Presence within.

It takes real persistence to move beyond these patterns of identity. It took years and even decades to form your egoic identity, your separate sense of self. Likewise, it takes time to unravel these patterns.

However, if you begin this process eventually the doorway of your Heart will open and you will fully experience the serene beauty of Loving Presence.

Always remember that it is of the utmost importance to focus on being present through your Heart. It is not about being present through your head or in some other part of your body. That simply will not cut it.

It is about being aware at the center of your being, which is the Heart and then allowing that awareness to spread throughout your entire existence.

By allowing each moment to be infused by the Loving Presence of the Heart, you are embracing and supporting the most effective and direct means possible to transform your life.

Beyond a shadow of a doubt you will successfully navigate, grow, and evolve through the maze of human existence. Then more happiness and peace will progressively unfold in your life.

The natural impulse of Consciousness is to grow and the most effective way to grow is through the experience of Loving Presence.

Loving Presence is the life force; it is the water that grows the tree. It is the energy that flows through every cell. Without it, we would just be a bunch of molecules going through a cellular biochemical process called life.

You have such great potential to grow into that radiant, Loving Presence. Then it can shine through your human form, touch other souls, and infuse them with the energy of enlightened Love.

It will also allow you to directly experience a state of peace and unity.

As you unfold and grow the Loving Presence in your Heart, your life and your spiritual journey will radically change for the better.

Then as the journey of the Heart progresses, more joy and happiness will emerge from deep within.

Loving Presence is the fuel and essence of who you truly are. It will lead you through the journey of life to true, lasting, love and happiness.

CHAPTER SIX

Seeing with New Eyes... Transcending Ego-Centricity

The expression "seeing with new eyes" is a way of saying that an individual can perceive something in their life, another person or situation from a new perspective.

This may be a perspective that the person was aware of, but never deeply considered, or it could be a perspective that is completely new.

As long as you keep seeing and experiencing life from the same habitual filters, you cannot have a different experience.

The focus of this book is unfolding The Awakened Heart. If you continue to see your life through the same filters, the Heart itself cannot grow and experience life in a new way.

To evolve your life, you need to cultivate a new perspective. In order to cultivate a new perspective you have to understand how you are viewing each moment.

As an individual you have become so used to functioning from a limited unaware perspective, that rarely do you consider the way you are seeing life, interpreting and experiencing it, is not Reality itself.

What you are seeing is simply your interpretation of Reality. To keep seeing your life with the same old eyes does not allow the deeper dimensions of who you are as a spiritual being to tangibly and palpably manifest.

This is due to the fact that part of your being has been squashed, confined and diminished by a limited perspective.

As you unfold in your spiritual journey, it is important to become aware of the concept of 'egocentricity'. By this, I mean that everything you have experienced in your life comes from the perspective that "you" as the ego, are the center of your life.

This viewpoint limits one's personal transformation because it does not allow for a greater insight into reality or allow you to see how you are creating your experience moment by moment.

As long as you continue to perceive life from an egocentric viewpoint, then you are constantly interpreting each moment through the filter of your conditioned ego.

A great example of this is the following: Before the advent of the telescope, astronomers and even the philosophy of the church stated with absolute conviction, that the earth was the center of our solar system and the sun and all the other planets revolved around it.

As far as everyone was concerned at the time, this made perfect sense. They were limited in their viewpoint because they only had very basic equipment and ideas regarding the solar system and how it worked.

This is the "I" perspective, the egocentric perspective in motion.

It is the belief that everything in existence revolves around oneself, that you are the center of everything that happens.

The problem with this perspective is that it is not Reality. As long as you are seeing with the eyes of the ego, you are obscuring reality as it really is.

You are constantly overlaying and filtering any experience you are having moment to moment with this egocentric viewpoint.

The ego is formed by everything you have experienced in your life. Those life experiences have formed your point of view and your sense of self, the little self, the ego self.

Your name, your history, your beliefs, your ideas, all form your ego identity. It is from this ego identity, that you perceive each moment.

From that conditioned viewpoint, whether you are having an experience in life that is pleasant or painful, it is experienced as if you are at the center of it; that it all revolves around you.

All of your thoughts, ideas, and feelings make up this ego pattern and create your unique perspective and interpretation of life.

Egocentricity keeps you from experiencing and seeing reality plainly and simply in its totality.

You cannot see the truth of what is because your reality is constantly filled up with everything that you identify yourself to be.

In truth, there is no fundamental center; there is no separate you, even though your experience is one of separateness and it appears to be validated though the five senses of the physical body.

A big part of the spiritual journey and evolution of the soul is to be able to see with a clear mind and an open heart. This is important so that you do not live life from the limitation of the egocentric perspective.

Changing this limited and limiting perspective is of the greatest importance, yet so many human beings live their life with a deep unquestioned conviction that everything they see, hear, think and feel, is Reality.

This inauthentic egocentric perspective is nothing more than a viewpoint yet individuals, religions and countries will fight and die for their viewpoint, for their interpretation of what is real.

You can readily see this occurring throughout mankind's history. The same ego principle at work in each individual can be expanded out and applied to corporations, religious institutions, governments, and so on.

They each see everything as revolving around themselves, as the center. As long as this viewpoint remains unquestioned or unchallenged then there is no possibility for authentic reality to be present in any moment.

It is the endless interpretations of the ego, be it individual or collective that maintains such a contracted limited experience of Reality.

The most important point to start with is to realize that your sense of self, the ego is merely a point of perception, a point of view. If you are taking your point of perception to be reality you cannot see with new eyes.

Seeing with New Eyes... Transcending Ego-Centricity

This seeing with the same old ego eyes is what creates karma for your personal spiritual journey. Karma is created by constantly repeating your individual ego patterns.

Until you wake up to the fact that your experience is merely a perspective, and not reality, you keep spinning the wheels of karma.

You keep creating action and reaction all of which maintains your inner experience in a state of turmoil and upheaval. I call this the sea of endless activity.

Every act and activity based on the egoic point of perception, churns the sea more.

It is an endless loop. The wheel of karma is self-perpetuating until you can see from another perspective. Until you realize that, "you" are not at the center of anything. It is only a viewpoint and is not founded on Reality itself.

When you do not automatically react to an experience that you are having, you allow an inner space and opening in which you can observe, see and feel how you normally react.

You can see how your interpretation of any arising experience creates a habitual response.

This habitual response to any situation, thought or event keeps the energy of the Heart contracted and your awareness self-limited.

In order to still the endless sea of egoic activity with its constant waves and motion, there has to be a pause. This pause is from the interpretation you are imposing on your current experience.

It creates space so that you can see and feel the moment as it really is thus allowing a transformation of your perception to take place.

In essence, enlightenment or freedom from the endless karmic wheel of life and death is really about changing your perspective at a fundamental level - from the perspective of the ego to authentic reality.

This is not something insurmountable. Anyone, if they choose can begin to unfold this in each moment. Simply watch how you interpret and react moment to moment.

Pause, to see if you are coming from an ego perspective. This pause can assist you to create a relaxed inner space that will allow you to feel more deeply into the subtle energies of the Heart.

In that pause, there is the possibility that the Heart can awaken, awareness expand and that Presence can manifest as an authentic, liberating experience for you.

When you connect to Presence in each moment, through the subtle doorway of the Heart, this process of ego-centricity that spurs action and reaction begins to quiet down.

If you do not catch yourself, the power of a single thought can stir up all kinds of emotions, feelings, and ideas and soon many moments have gone by and you have not been present at all.

It is easy to see how your egocentric viewpoint, which is made up of thousands of thoughts, emotional feelings and sensations, is an absolutely convincing alternative to Reality.

This ego viewpoint effectively limits your ability to experience Presence.

The senses, through which we experience human life, are always a modified, limited filter of reality as it really is.

Everything that we see with our eyes is only one perspective and is filtered through our minds.

Many animals see in different ways than we do because their brain interprets the electrical impulses through the eyes differently.

For example, some animals can see in infrared. This allows them to see in darkness. In addition, many animals have much wider peripheral vision than we do thus allowing them to see much more than we can.

It is the same with our hearing. The low range of human hearing is around twenty hertz and the high range twenty thousand hertz. We are unable to hear any noise outside that range.

Yet, Elephants can communicate with other elephants over a mile away using low-pitched vibrational sounds that are well outside our range of hearing. Just because you cannot hear it does not mean it is not there.

The same thing applies with the sense of smell. It is a well-known fact that dogs can pick up on scents and track those scents over long distances.

We only experience a certain fraction of what is actually available to be experienced through our senses, yet we take that limited experience to be the totality of reality.

It goes unquestioned.

It is important that you consider and contemplate the ways in which your experience of life is limited.

It is limited because your viewpoint is so engrained and second nature to you. Therefore, you take it for granted as being Truth rather than simply a conditioned viewpoint that is based on your own mind and your life experiences.

Be willing to pause from the chaos of the mind and your emotional energetic experiences so that you can perceive and experience with "New Eyes". This allows for the possibility of a new perspective to arise.

The shift from the perspective of egocentricity begins with the understanding that what you see, feel, hear, and think is only a limited perspective in relation to what actually is.

An important stage within the spiritual journey is to wake up from your ego perspective, because egocentricity is what separates you from the Divine Reality of Loving Presence.

There has to be an awakening to a Greater Intelligence and this is not the intelligence of the mind, it is the intelligence of Consciousness.

No amount of mental thinking will allow you to arrive at that point. This greater opening can only be experienced in the Heart Space of here and now.

You make space for this opening to happen firstly by being present, attentive, and aware of your Heart.

Secondly by being aware that your normal way of perceiving and experiencing life is a limited version of what is.

Another useful understanding is the realization that your behavior is deeply motivated by the egocentric viewpoint. This insight into your ego behavior can be very liberating indeed.

The ego functions from two primary motives. The first motive is to seek and experience pleasure and happiness.

The second motive is to avoid painful experiences. Of course, the ultimate experience of pain for an individual ego is death.

These two underlying motives are constantly driving a person's life and behavior as a separate ego.

These motivations are what keep the sea of karmic activity churning and the wheels of karma spinning. Therefore, it is very important and useful to have insight into how your individual ego functions.

Without this insight, you will most likely continue to act and live in a very robotic and unconscious manner. Then it is very difficult if not impossible to find inner stillness.

When you connect with that inner stillness a natural shift occurs in relation to the experience that you are having in the moment and therefore to your perception or point of view also.

There is movement away from the mental processes of the mind and into a greater space of Awareness and Heart Presence.

In that moment, your inner sourceful Presence has the space to arise and to change your experience of the moment.

Experiences of Sourcefull presence and awareness are always felt as a greater sense of love and peace, innate joy and happiness.

None of these Source-Full experiences are caused by something you have done or have received or by any event that is happening.

They exist beyond the perceptions of the ego and its normal process of action and reaction.

Thus, one key objective in life is to arrive at this pure Awakened Heart experience which has nothing to do with the limited egoic point of view.

It is simply the un-filtered experience of Reality.

Here is a simple exercise from an Eastern tradition that is helpful in beginning this process. Just take each thought and feeling and label it as it arises.

For example, you enter a room and see a chair:

Rather than allow the act of seeing the chair to trigger off other ideas or concerns about the chair - is it soft, is it comfortable, do I want to sit in it now or later - you just say, "Seeing".

If you notice the mind still wants to attach a whole string of thoughts and ideas to the chair just come back to "seeing".

If you hear a noise, just say "Hearing". Then wait and see if that creates a pause. If it does, just be in the space and stillness of the pause. Relax into the Presence that can be felt in that pause.

Notice that stillness has no ego or viewpoint. Notice the ego is in fact a type of illusion. Like a mirage, it is not really there as a solid sense of self.

What lies beneath this ego mirage, is Awareness, Presence and Consciousness. This is what you are attempting to connect to on your spiritual journey.

This connection to what Reality truly Is, will most certainly occur by "transcending your limited ego identity and seeing with new eyes".

CHAPTER SEVEN

The Sacred Trinity... Body, Mind and Heart-Spirit

In Western religion, the Holy Trinity is referred to as "The Father, Son and Holy Ghost". The term "Sacred Trinity" that I am using in this book has a different meaning and purpose. Please do not confuse these two terms for they are entirely different from one another.

The Sacred Trinity, unlike the Holy Trinity, is not just an abstract religious concept or idea. It is that which makes up the very foundation of your human life experience.

The Sacred Trinity is the cornerstone of human transformation. It is your Body, in which you are living and breathing, your Mind and all the thoughts and ideas that pass through it, and your Heart-Spirit which includes the vast assortment of human emotional experience.

Very simply put the Sacred Trinity is Body, Mind and Heart-Spirit.

Rather than use the term "Spirit" in the traditional way, I am using the term Heart-Spirit because it is the Heart that governs spirit.

The essence of Spirit is energy also referred to as chi, or prana. Spirit is the conscious life energy that lives and animates the human body.

In terms of your spiritual transformational unfolding, the Sacred Trinity is of the greatest importance.

It is through the Sacred Trinity of the Body, Mind, and Heart-Spirit that you grow and unfold your human spiritual life.

The Sacred Trinity is how you will bring your soul to a greater state of Awakening within this lifetime. Your mastery and awakening will not be found in an external place such as a church, temple or monastery.

Wherever you go all that you need for your greater liberation and happiness is the Sacred Trinity of your very own Body, Mind and Heart-Spirit.

The sacred temple is your body and it is the alchemical vessel in which the great work of spiritual transformation occurs. To unfold spiritually you need to work with these three fundamental dimensions.

A useful analogy here is that of a large ocean liner:

There are a number of requirements for an ocean liner to function on the high seas. Firstly, it needs a captain to direct the ship and to make sure the right course has been set.

In this analogy the captain of your spiritual journey across the ocean of human experience, is your mind.

For the spiritual journey, you need a mind that is clear, focused and filled with Sourceful intelligence as well as the wisdom and know how to arrive at your intended destination.

The destination of the spiritual journey is referred to as Enlightenment. Enlightenment of the Soul begins to unfold as the three primary dimensions of Body, Mind and Heart-Spirit come into relative harmony and balance.

Secondly, a ship needs a powerful engine in order to propel it across the endless miles of ocean to its final destination.

In the human body, the Heart-Spirit is the engine that powers us and gives us the energy to make our spiritual voyage. Therefore, our Heart-Spirit needs to be strong and in sound working order.

The more emotional heartbreaks and pains that an individual experiences throughout their life, the weaker will be the overall energetic strength of their Heart-Spirit.

Just like any engine it eventually needs an overhaul, which for human beings is emotional energetic healing and inner repair work.

Inner emotional healing of the Heart requires great persistence and the willingness to heal various energetic wounds that for many people may be decades old.

Lastly, there is the ship itself, which in our human experience is the physical body. An ocean liner needs to be sea worthy; it cannot be filled with holes. The Body is made strong though proper exercise, rest, nutrition and breathing practices.

An ocean liner has to be sea-worthy to go through all the storms, challenges, and conditions the ocean can throw at it. The physical body has to be equally sound and balanced so that the journey of Awakening can be undertaken and progressively unfolded throughout one's lifetime.

This Sacred Trinity of Body, Mind and Heart-Spirit is critical in the undertaking of our personal spiritual quest to awaken and discover that which lies within the depths of our very own "Beingness".

To summarize: You need a clear mind to give your life direction. You need an open, strong heart to give you energy for that journey and lastly you need a physical body that can endure all the rigors and challenges that lie ahead of you.

Each of these dimensions, your Body, Mind and Heart-Spirit, is really a sacred treasure. Let's briefly explore and examine how we can cultivate, transform and evolve each of these areas.

The physical body is comprised of many bio-chemical processes. In order for the physical body to be nurtured, you need to make sure you are putting life giving food and nutrients into it, on a daily basis.

From life comes life so it is with the food that you eat. If it is vital, raw, natural and organic you are providing the best fuel for your body.

The body has certain energetic and nutritional requirements if it is going to perform at optimal levels and not become diseased before it has completed its purpose of Awakening.

To ensure the body will be a strong vessel for the voyage you have to nurture its development and ongoing transformation.

Many people do not realize that the transformation of limiting ego patterns requires a tremendous amount of energy and vitality.

The Sacred Trinity... Body, Mind and Heart-Spirit

The vital energy of the physical body must be cultivated over time so that it grows and strengthens, rather than weakens and withers which is the case for most people as they get older.

If you are not strong and healthy now, remember that the physical body can be regenerated, rejuvenated, and consciously cultivated to function at an ever-greater level of health and vitality.

This healing and balancing can begin once you understand that the food you eat the air you breathe, the water you drink and the lifestyle you live have a direct impact on whether your body is being strengthened or weakened.

In addition to nutrition, there are practices such as Yoga and Qigong that help to open up the energy channels of the body. These assist in creating a smooth flow of life force energy, prana, or Chi.

These practices help energy to move through the physical body and the subtle energy body in a very smooth and fluid way. The physical body is a sacred treasure and constitutes one dimension of your Temple of Being.

Next is the dimension of Mind. From the time we are little children we are educated. We go to school and learn the basics in math, writing, English, social studies, and so on.

All of these classes are considered mandatory yet for the most part; we are not exposed to Sourceful Life Wisdom that teaches us about the spiritual journey and the unfolding of our inner spiritual potential.

A captain in charge of navigating a ship across the ocean needs to have an excellent knowledge of the terrain. Likewise we each need to have inner spiritual knowledge and wisdom to help us progress in our spiritual unfolding.

This knowledge and wisdom is of vital necessity in order to successfully cross the endless inner terrain that we will each face.

We will require a different type of education than the usual training we get in school and college. Travelling the inner terrain requires a different set of skills and abilities that allow us to focus in a new way that is based upon an understanding of our human spiritual journey.

For this, the mind needs to be cultivated and filled with real knowledge that overtime leads to the development of spiritual wisdom.

An essential component of developing the mind spiritually has to do with the ability to focus it like a laser. The ability to focus the mind in a useful way is essential to developing insight that leads to wisdom.

There are many different ways to go about this. Reading the great sacred texts from different spiritual traditions whether they be Christian, Buddhist, or Hindu is just one example of how to focus and develop the mind in a useful way.

Aside from the ability to focus the mind, there must also be a strong intention to be alert and present to the thoughts and patterns that are arising.

The Sacred Trinity... Body, Mind and Heart-Spirit

This intention is necessary in order to continually cultivate the mind with spiritual wisdom regarding your personal limiting life-conditioning.

This is important because it will give you a greater capacity to deal with the various challenges that you will encounter in your life.

The last primary dimension of this Sacred Trinity is the Heart. To return to our analogy of the ocean liner, the Heart is that part of us that fuels and propels our vessel, the human body, to its destination.

Therefore, the Heart must be cultivated as a treasure. We all know the Heart's most important fundamental quality is love. Love is the fuel that powers the engine of the Heart.

As you go throughout your life, if you are not experiencing love or giving and sharing love, then the primary fuel for your Heart is not there to draw on.

Without love, the Heart cannot grow and evolve into all that it can be. If the Heart does not learn to grow in love it becomes a grave yard rather than a sanctuary for spiritual transformation.

Each of these three aspects of your Being is a treasure. If properly cultivated and tended over the decades of your human life, they will assist in creating the progressive transformation and evolution of your soul.

Developing the Sacred Trinity will allow you to travel further and deeper into the dimensions of Consciousness and the realms of Source-Filled Reality. This is the journey of unfolding your divine human potential.

The intention within each of one our souls, is to unfold more and more of who we are as Consciousness.

In order to do this, our physical body needs to be sound, our heart needs to be strong and fueled by the energy of love and our mind must be clear, focused and filled with spiritual wisdom.

These three primary dimensions can be cultivated using a specific process that I call "The Sacred Trinity Process". Each one of these three dimensions, Body, Mind and Heart-Spirit, is connected to and reflected in an aspect of our physical body.

The physical body is represented most directly by the breath. Breathing is necessary for life and each breath holds within it, prana, a subtle energy that rides on each breath and is the energy of Consciousness.

Bring your awareness to the solar plexus area (where the diaphragm resides) and to the abdominal region and notice the energy that is there.

By doing this you can gain valuable insight into what is happening in your whole body. Check and see if your abdominal area is open and relaxed or tight and contracted.

Is your breath rhythmic and even throughout the day or is it shallow and unconscious?

The Sacred Trinity... Body, Mind and Heart-Spirit

Becoming aware of your breath especially in the regions of the solar plexus and the abdomen is the first part of the Sacred Trinity Process.

Most people are totally unconscious to the fact that their abdomen is tight. This indicates chronic tension and blockage of the subtle life force energy throughout the body.

The next dimension of the Sacred Trinity Process is the mind. As you go throughout your day, bring your awareness to your mind.

What are you thinking? What kinds of thoughts are going through your mind? Are they negative, limiting, and self-destructive or are they positive and life affirming?

Is your mind flowing with spiritual thoughts and full of wisdom that has to do with your growth and transformation? Or are you caught up in worrying about something in your past or what might happen in the future?

Becoming aware of what is happening in your mind moment by moment is the second part of the Sacred Trinity Process.

Most people's minds are chronically and continuously lost in a sea of thoughts and beliefs that overlay each moment of experience.

As long as you are lost in your thoughts, it is not possible to be Present and Aware.

The last aspect of the Sacred Trinity Process has to do with your Heart. Be aware of the feelings you are having. Are your feelings joyful, happy, and loving or are they feelings of stress, anxiety, and fear?

Is your Heart and the region around it, tight, constricted and guarded?

By becoming aware of your Heart, you can see what is happening with your emotions and feelings.

Remember, it is the Heart that governs the overall energy of the body. If your Heart is blocked, contracted and stressed then your overall experience will be one of stress, limitation, and separateness.

The Sacred Trinity Process is something to be aware of in each moment. It is something you can do as a simple practice wherever you find yourself throughout the day.

This is how you begin the process of cultivating real and authentic Wisdom about yourself and your spiritual journey.

No one can give you this wisdom it is up to you to cultivate it step by step.

When you are out and about you can scan what is happening with your breath, what you are feeling in your Heart, and what thoughts are going through your mind.

By doing this, you are bringing awareness to the Sacred Trinity of Body, Mind, and Heart-Spirit and seeing how balanced each of these are in the present moment.

The transformational journey is about cultivating harmony and balance and your journey is greatly assisted when you bring your attention to this process.

The more you can align and harmonize your Body, Mind, and Heart-Spirit, the more they work together in unity.

The Sacred Trinity... Body, Mind and Heart-Spirit

This is a synergistic process that will allow your inner spiritual journey to unfold in the most direct, efficient and magical way possible.

Most people are totally lost and consumed by their life, their work, their relationship etc.

Because of this, they are not aware of their breath in each moment nor are they aware of and sensitized to the deeper dimensions of their Heart.

For the most part, they are not focused on cultivating loving presence nor is it even possible because they are unconscious to what is happening within their very own Body, Mind, and Heart-Spirit.

This is why it is so important to bring equal awareness to each of these primary dimensions of the human spiritual journey.

Cultivating the Sacred Trinity is a great responsibility as well as an absolute necessity for those who wish to proceed effectively on their spiritual path.

This is tending to the Sacred Temple of Being which is always reflected right here and now, through your Body, your Mind and your Heart.

One last relevant thought for you to consider; everything that is shared in this book is only useful if you apply it.

There is a saying: "Action without wisdom is blind and wisdom without action is sterile".

If you are doing things in life and acting and reacting without any underlying wisdom to your actions, then those actions are unconscious and blind. They cannot produce anything of significance in terms of your deeper spiritual transformation.

Likewise if you have wisdom but you do not act upon it and make appropriate changes to transform your life, then that wisdom is useless. It is nothing more than a series of thoughts that blow around like dust in the wind.

So as you continue your journey of unfolding, cultivate and develop the Temple of your Being through the Sacred Trinity of Body, Mind, and Heart-Spirit.

Stay grounded and Present and your journey will unfold in its own unique timing, within the universal play of Reality.

CHAPTER EIGHT

Finding Authentic Love through Presence

At the core of our emotional and psychological conditioning, is a deep wound of the Heart. This wound has to do with feeling "separate". The feeling of separateness goes back to our earliest beginnings as a small infant.

When a child is in the womb, there exists a sense of unity that is whole and complete. From the moment of birth, the child bonds with the mother and thus establishes a sense of unity and love with the outer world.

As the baby grows, there are moments of separation from the mother. Since the baby links its mother with feelings of love and union, being separated is extremely painful and feels to the infant like being separated from love itself.

Thus at the very core of our emotional and psychological makeup is this deep primal wound of separateness, created in our earliest infancy.

Therefore, we approach life from an already inherited viewpoint and belief that we are separate from love itself.

From that point on, so much of our life revolves around an effort to find the union-experience of love. A huge part of our journey is formed around the effort to connect with love and the feeling of Oneness.

Our life is formulated and driven by the impulse to seek unity which is the experience of love.

The irony is that the psychological model of a baby, who is dependent on another to give it love and attention, is a model that cannot ultimately create a lasting experience of love and Oneness.

It becomes a never ending, unfulfilling experience. No matter how much love the child receives from the mother, it is never enough because in any given moment there is an underlying fear that this love can be lost or taken away.

This creates a deep energetic, emotional and physiological disturbance within each of us. As we grow up, we continue to play out this pattern of expecting to receive love from outside our self.

Many of the motivations we have and the desires that drive our behavior come from this attempt to seek union with the mother (the object) with whom we associate the experience of love.

In depth psychology they refer to this as "object relations", in Eastern spiritual systems it is known as "a state of duality".

The state of duality always requires a subject (the individual) and an object, which could be your mother or father or as you grow older, your partner, your son or your daughter.

When you live a life based on duality, there is always the possibility that love can be lost. This sets up a myriad of emotional and psychological triggers that can catalyze you in any moment.

For example, loving someone can create fear of rejection. What if I give him/her all my love and I am not loved in return? This fear generates defensive patterns in an attempt to prevent the possibility of rejection.

All of this creates stress and anxiety, which may even cause the fear to become a reality.

Jealousy is another common pattern. You become jealous about what the one you love is doing and jealous when his or her attention is given to another.

Jealousy creates the fear that the other could love someone else more than you and thus the whole relationship could end leaving you very vulnerable.

The feeling of vulnerability can create behavioral patterns of scheming and manipulation in the attempt to maintain the love relationship.

Underlying all of these behaviors is the constant fear that the person you love may not love you anymore or that the quality of that love will change.

When you do not experience enough love from the other you may try to get the other persons attention through negative behavior.

The attention given back, in the eyes of the person who is seeking it, is interpreted as "being loved". Another strategy is to simply shut down and withdraw your love from the other out of fear that the loss of love is imminent.

Reflect on your behavior and look at your patterns to see how this model of Dualistic love is playing out in your personal life. Also observe other people as it is easier to see these underlying psychological emotional patterns in someone else than to see your own.

As long as an individual is attempting to seek love, they cannot actually discover love and this is the big irony and the catch twenty-two of life.

As long as you believe that love is something separate from you, then on some emotional psychological level of your being the need to find and acquire love will drive your patterns of behavior.

It will drive your sense of how you perceive life and your personal experiences.

The great challenge and difficulty of this deep emotional wound and behavioral pattern is that it creates trauma and stress within the deeper subtle energetic dimensions of the Heart. Then these dimensions recoil and actually shut down very much like a camera lens.

When a camera lens is wide open it lets the light in fully but when the shutter starts to close, light begins to diminish. This is what happens to pretty much every individual soul; they become removed from the actual dimension and experience of inner love and light.

Once you are no longer in the experience of love within yourself, you are caught in the dualistic model of yourself as a subject and love as the object. Then, the subject has to acquire the object.

Finding Authentic Love through Presence

The subject has to acquire and get love from another person in order to feel happy, to feel satisfied, and to feel complete, even though this is merely a temporary solution to the problem.

Unfortunately, this is a fruitless endeavor because it is not based on reality. It is based on emotional psychological conditioning within the developmental unfolding of the individual.

These deep energetic imprints remain unless the individual undertakes a journey of healing, clearing and awakening.

This emotional psychological conditioning is imprinted in the Heart and to a certain extent throughout the entire body-mind structure.

There can be no genuine, lasting experience of peace and happiness and certainly no experience of love that is permanent, until you Awaken beyond the experience of duality.

There will be moments when you experience reflections of love, and experience some aspect of love, but this is not the full and complete experience. It is not the totality of love.

Until you are able to simply be present and to be love, you will always be motivated to seek that which you already are and this is the great irony of the whole spiritual journey.

There is a lot of talk in spiritual circles that tells people they are "love, eternal spiritual consciousness, bliss, and peace".

Yes all of this is true but until you heal and clear whatever is obstructing that from being apparent and from being self-obvious to you in the moment, then these statements of truth are not true for you.

They are simply words of truth.

The reality is most people are unable to be experientially present to Love. There is simply too much in the way in terms of emotional and psychological energetic imprints, to allow love to flow and be experienced in the present moment.

The Heart is innately structured to flow love and this is its real purpose and function.

In the world when a new house is being built, if the structure isn't properly put into place then the house cannot fulfill its designed purpose.

So it is with the Heart. When there is emotional and psychological obstruction to the free flow of love from the Heart, its purpose cannot be fulfilled.

Life is really a process of uncovering and healing everything that is obstructing the love and presence that you already are.

Once that healing has taken place then love and presence begin to radiate quite naturally in an effortless way.

It is not something that you have to scheme about or manipulate in order to achieve. It is something that is innate and as natural as the air around us.

Air is available to us all but we have to breathe. Love is available to us all but we have to go through the process of healing the primal wound of the Heart, the wound of separateness.

If you do not undertake this journey then the body, the emotions, the mind and psyche will go through a process of calcification.

On a physical level, calcification occurs when calcium in the body begins to harden over time in the blood vessels and arteries and from there moves into the heart, joints, and ligaments.

It is the process of the body becoming cemented. This process occurs in our emotional and psychological patterns also.

That is why most people, who do not intentionally and consciously work on themselves, will eventually experience calcification within their Body, Mind, and Heart-Spirit.

Once the calcification sets in place it is just like putting up a wall – it will not remove itself unless you work to dismantle it.

For the most part once a person's ego personality - which is their experience of themselves emotionally, psychologically and mentally - is set in place, then that is it.

The calcification has occurred and the subtler dimensions of the Spiritual Heart have no avenue for manifestation.

This means there is no openness for the dimension of Consciousness that we call love, to flow through and into our normal everyday existence as a human being.

Therefore, if you do not want to live your entire life in a subject/object dualistic way, constantly in search of love, then you must embrace the healing and clearing of these self-limiting emotional psychological patterns.

Otherwise, you make yourself dependent upon the outer world and the "other" person in order to experience love.

The journey of healing this deep primal wound is an important undertaking. The first step in any process is to start with the truth.

In this case, the truth can simply be expressed in an affirmation "I am love". Looking for someone or something outside yourself to give you love is not based on spiritual reality.

It is based on an obstruction within your own being that keeps you from experiencing this stated truth: "I am Love".

The first step in the quest to heal these deeper dimensions of your Heart and psyche is to remind yourself that you are love through inner affirmation. This is best done while in meditation.

The next step is to take moments throughout your day to slow down, stop, and just be. You have to allow space for the experience of love to manifest.

Most people are so distracted, and so stressed with the "busyness" of their lives they never create the space for love to manifest. Thus creating space for love to arise is the second step.

The third step is to recognize that this is really a lifelong process. It is not something you can just go out and get and once you have acquired it, that's the end of the process.

To think in this way is to be out of alignment with reality and how it manifests in a human body on this physical plane.

Finding Authentic Love through Presence

The truth is that each individual soul is in an eternally unfolding process of growth and transformation. Therefore you are not going to somehow get or acquire love, and then that's it.

It is a lifelong process and the Heart, like the shutter on a camera lens, progressively learns how to open more frequently and for longer periods of time.

This lens opens into the deeper dimensions of your Heart, to Consciousness, to the infinite dimensions of reality that are unending, eternal and lie deep within you.

If you have certain emotional psychological challenges then these will need to be addressed and healed, so that your Heart can be set free to naturally radiate the love that it is.

Any aspects of your personality that are out of alignment will need to be brought back into balance. This will allow for your inner transformation to continue in a holistic manner.

Most of us put on a social face that covers any inner feelings of unhappiness and pain. Instead of owning up to how we feel in an honest and upfront way we put on a face of non-vulnerability.

We do not allow ourselves to be vulnerable to the deeper truth of what we are feeling or to see it as an appropriate aspect of unraveling and healing our wounded Heart.

As you continue in this journey of healing and transformation, you will eventually experience more openness, more energy and a greater loving presence flowing through your Heart and throughout your entire body.

This is the love that you are. This is the love that so many people seek.

A very important part of the spiritual journey is to grow, transform and heal this primal Heart wound of separateness. Then you can progressively live your life from the place of being love itself.

When you live your life from the place of being love, the stress and the tension that is wrapped up in the wounded emotional, psychological patterns is set free.

Then your Soul can truly be happy and at peace in each moment of your life.

This process takes place over time and unfolds with your conscious intention. Then, instead of living from a sense of effort, you start to live life as a flow from a space of peace and a state of joy and love.

Remember, that you are Love and let that be your mantra in moments when you find yourself not living this eternal Truth.

CHAPTER NINE

The Sometimes Arduous Journey of Being Love

Many people think (the operative word being "think") they are loving human beings. However, what you discover as you become more awake and more spiritually aware is that there are many dimensions and stages of love.

As the chapter heading states, it is an arduous journey to Being Love, but the rewards of inner joy and peace are well worth the effort.

Let's explore together a deeper understanding of why it is so difficult for human beings to completely love from the depths of their Spiritual Heart.

To start with most people are unconscious to the fact that they do not fully love. This is due to numerous causes, one of which is traumatic and painful experiences they have had in the past.

These painful and sometimes horrendous experiences make it difficult for a person to flow love and to be present in life as love.

Thus, the arduous part of this journey is learning how to work through those parts of ourselves that are out of alignment with love. These aspects keep us from a greater spiritual unfolding and from deepening our spiritual journey.

Once our personality or ego-self has solidified, it is rare that a human being operates from the deeper dimensions of love, unless life circumstances thrust a new challenge upon them that creates an opening in their Heart and awareness.

Nonetheless, the fuel for our spiritual journey is in fact love itself and if we are unable to love, we remain cut off from the fuel and energy that is necessary for us to transform.

Once an individual reaches this level of ego solidification, it is very difficult for any further transformation to take place.

To successfully grow in love it is important to understand the two primary energies operating within every human being.

The first energy wants to maintain the individual as they currently are. This energy is really one of stagnation. It wants to keep everything the same and does not want to explore anything that may make one feel uncomfortable or stressed in anyway.

This creates stagnation within a person's spiritual develop-ment, and in the unfolding of more subtle states of Consciousness. Stagnation is one way the ego operates in order to maintain control over the sense of self.

The ego wants the same ice-cream every day; it wants the same relationship, the same job, it wants to do the same thing in order to have the same experience and so on.

However, having the same experience day in and day out does not lead one to inner liberation and happiness. The impulse of the ego to stay the same does not open the doorways to the totality of who we are as Consciousness.

Therefore, the potential for experiencing joy, happiness, and love greatly diminishes.

There is great potential for every human being to flower and awaken spiritually.

However, if they do not move beyond this pattern of the ego that wants to stagnate and resist change, then they will only experience fleeting glimpses of their inner light and spiritual potential.

The second energy is the impulse to grow. After you have been doing the same thing day in and day out, it begins to get a little boring. It starts to be void of any real joy or vital energy and there is a lack of enthusiasm and excitement.

Beneath the impulse to stay the same, lays the impulse that wants to grow. This deep impulse is the impulse of Consciousness, the impulse that created the universe. It is the creative impulse or energy also referred to as Eros.

If Consciousness were happy to simply be Consciousness, it would have no necessity to create the manifest world and the billions of stars and galaxies that exist.

All of these manifestations arise because there is an impulse in Consciousness to become a living Self-Conscious, Self-Aware Being that can experience itself through human and myriad other forms.

In order to have "experience" there had to be the creation of various life forms. If everything simply remained in the black soup of infinite space with no light and no planets or galaxies, there would be no-thing to create contrast.

There would also be no human beings to reflect on and experience divine Consciousness and Presence.

We are each made of the same Consciousness that has this impulse to create the known universe and to fully experience itself. Thus there is an impulse inside each human being to unfold one's inner spiritual potential and to fully flower.

This impulse resides deep within the Heart of each being. Yet, as we grow and develop within our current body, we forget this impulse to a large degree.

The impulse to grow spiritually and to actualize ever-greater potential becomes progressively covered over by the development of the ego and one's experiences in life.

Our life becomes a persona driven reality that is unaware of its greater purpose. We become Unconscious. We become limited, confined, and imprisoned by the ego identity.

A racing car is a sophisticated machine and requires pure, highly refined fuel in order to perform optimally at a very high level.

The human body is also a sophisticated machine with the potential to operate on very pure subtle energy. This is the energy of unconditional love.

However, in general the energy we live on is not the one hundred percent pure life force that arises from the deeper dimensions of an open Heart.

Instead, we live off the derivatives of this energy: the food we eat the air we breathe etc. The Heart itself remains in a cocoon waiting for the potential metamorphosis that for most people never comes.

The fuel that gives energy to our spiritual life is experienced as pure love. Have you ever experienced that energy of pure love?

This is the love you feel when you first meet someone that you have a deep energetic connection with before you experience all of your personal issues and the conflicts that arise.

There is just a pure energy of love. It is such a palpable, powerful energy. It is divinely nourishing and sustaining on the levels of body, mind and soul. With it comes such inner states as De-Light, Happiness and Contentment.

However, because we are not consciously educated about how to sustain and grow in love, it very quickly recedes. Thus the challenge is how to continue to grow spiritually and how to "grow" our Heart?

The Heart is the great balancer in spiritual growth – it guides us to unfold spiritually in a balanced way.

It is possible to have psychic experiences, subtle energy experiences, visions and visit beautiful worlds. However if your Heart is not in the driver's seat of your spiritual journey then your soul will unfold in an imbalanced way.

Imbalance shows itself in the form of stress, unhappiness and things not flowing right in your life. That is okay. It is just an indication that you are not living from the deeper awareness and presence of the Awakened Heart.

For the most part, living from that place is impossible for people because their spiritual Heart is no longer accessible to their conscious mind. It is covered by layers of stress and tension.

Unless a person finds a way to remove and soften these layers of stress, which lead to disease and unhappiness, they continue to grow and harden. For the most part this is an unconscious process and happens very gradually over many months and years of a person's life.

Thus the Heart becomes hardened and covered over time. Because of this, the majority of people are not aware of their current condition. They do not know that they are fundamentally disconnected and cut off.

This disconnection makes it difficult for a person to love fully and completely, in any present moment. Thus love becomes an ego driven search rather than an innately born aspect of ourselves.

When life is lived purely from the view point of the ego, then there is a disconnect and an inability to sense and feel with the Heart.

Therefore, an individual's life choices will be made by their limited unaware ego. This has tremendous consequences in terms of unfolding one's ability to keep the Heart open and loving.

If you are really interested in spiritual transformation, and want to evolve your divine human potential then there will come a point where the "arduous" part of "learning to love", will become blatantly apparent to you.

If you make a commitment to love, if you make a commitment to your spiritual transformation, you have to realize that involves making some real changes.

It is not about having the idea "Oh, I am going to be a loving person" or "I want to experience love and have a loving life" it involves real changes.

It is very difficult to change one's egoic structures because the personality-self has solidified from an early age. It requires inner work at a very deep level to make a difference.

It is one thing to say "I would like to be a millionaire" and another thing to commit to work for another thirty years, give up your free time and other things that you enjoy in your life, in order to turn the dream of that intention into an actual reality.

What it comes down to many times, is that most people do not really want to commit to giving up their ego identity and the limitation that goes with it. It is easier to stay the same. Again this is the stagnation part of the ego.

The truth is that once you begin to spiritually transform it can be arduous and uncomfortable.

This is made even more difficult if you do not have someone who is personally guiding you through the inner challenges that lay ahead.

Let's say you begin this work within your Heart and choose to look at some emotional belief patterns that have been limiting you and creating suffering in your life.

You may notice as you start this process that what arises is a subtle level of resistance to exploring and feeling that issue more deeply. This is where the spiritual "rubber" meets the transformational "road".

This is where you are tested and challenged. Are you willing to make that change in order to grow? Are you willing to go through the pain and discomfort that comes with change?

Are you willing to explore the deep dark inner recesses of your mental emotional patterns? Are you ready to confront those things in yourself that disgust you and create knots in your stomach?

You have to remember that the Heart is the most sensitive dimension of your being. This is both a blessing and a curse in many ways. Your Heart can easily be injured and will naturally withdraw from any experience that is less than loving.

If it feels the slightest pain it will naturally withdraw and shutdown from feeling any deeper. Avoiding pain is part of our ego structure for self-preservation, but this same tendency to avoid feeling pain can and does usually become one's inner prison.

It is one's awareness that withdraws from the pain. The irony of course is that without awareness you cannot transform your life negative limiting patterns.

The question then becomes are you willing to make life changes that may be painful?

For example would you be willing to change your beliefs or your self-image? What if the change required was on a physical level?

Would you be willing to change your diet and balance your biochemistry in order to keep your energy open and flowing so that more love can flow through your Heart?

Change may be required in many areas of your life. To be the love that you are and to exist as that love, requires the real transformation of who you are as an egoic conditioned human being.

Otherwise, the ego is blocking the development of the more subtle spiritual dimensions.

The subtle nature of who you are as a loving, feeling spiritual being is easily affected by the dysfunctional, diseased, distressed, and disharmonious energies of the imbalanced human personality.

These imbalances can easily block the greater awakening and transformation of your soul.

The Heart is very much like a delicate flower. Even though the Heart is ultimately a powerful and beautiful energy it can be easily destroyed or damaged by intense energies.

Like an orchid, it needs to have the right conditions in order to unfold its beauty and to flourish.

You need to always maintain awareness of where you are at in your journey and be able to feel how your current life situation is affecting your ability to love fully and completely.

Utilize the following exercise when you want to connect with the love in your Heart. When you experience Love, it makes it easier and more tolerable to transform those dimensions that may be deemed less than desirable.

First thing to be aware of is that the Heart and the eyes are energetically linked - the eyes being "the window of the soul".

A simple way to connect with the Heart energy of Love is to imagine your eyes smiling. Feel the inner relaxation of the smile in the muscles surrounding your eyes.

When you smile with your eyes, you can feel and experience a certain delight coming out of them. This makes it easier to then open and feel the Heart.

Feel that joy and then connect that sense of delight with the energy of delight in the Heart. Now let the Heart smile like a big Cheshire cat grinning from ear to ear.

Let the feeling of delight expand throughout your whole body. Then let that inner smile radiance spread throughout your entire body as you allow yourself to luxuriate in this space for several moments.

This exercise helps to soften and connect the inner energy channels. Try this in moments throughout your day so that you get used to connecting the energy of the Heart with the energy of the eyes.

As you do this over time, the energy channel that runs from the Heart core to the brain will open wider and allow more loving energy to flow into the present moment.

Another useful self-check to use throughout the day, is to see if you are flowing love or if that flow is blocked. If there is a blockage, ask yourself, "How am I blocking love in this moment?" See what is there.

If a situation arises and you feel anger, you will notice that the anger is blocking love. There is no way that you can be loving and be angry at the same time. Love is the energy of expansion and relaxation and anger is one of contraction and stress.

Noticing that you are angry is a starting point to reflect on the patterns you are choosing to animate. Next, look at the effect they have on you.

If you are blocking love, you are blocking your own spiritual transformation and not contributing positively to the situation or to the awakening of Consciousness on the planet.

Therefore, your experience, choices and actions in the moment have a great impact on what you create in your life.

Knowing this you can look at what is driving your life and motivating your actions. Notice and ask, "Is this cultivating my Heart or is it stopping my Heart from opening in this present moment?"

If the answer is "yes, it is stopping my Heart from opening", then you are confronting an obstruction to your ability to Love. Therefore, it will require focus and work on your part to solve the current riddle at hand.

These are a few very simple but useful tools to start you in the right direction. You cannot change what you are not aware of – noticing an obstruction is the first step to changing it.

As you continue your spiritual unfolding you will keep growing and progressively become more and more loving. This is your true nature.

Yes, this journey will at times be arduous but the rewards of learning to love and eventually being able to Be Love will bring you the authentic happiness and peace that you are deeply thirsting for.

CHAPTER TEN

Unfolding your Spiritual Destiny
Through Insight and Understanding

A critical part of the spiritual journey is developing the ability to delve into those parts of yourself that are limiting and preventing growth to greater Heart Presence, love and awareness.

Thus self-understanding and insight into your inner structure and workings of your Body, Mind and Spirit will become a critical component to successfully transforming your life from top to bottom.

Most people never go to any internal level of depth in relation to their emotional, mental patterns, nor do they practice self-reflection, contemplation and meditation which would lead to life transforming insight and understanding about their spiritual journey.

In general, people's attention and awareness are locked into a very repetitive level of experience that does not allow the space and time for contemplation and consideration to occur.

For the most part they do not go beyond the normal aspects of life to reflect on a deeper level about their personal patterns, beliefs and attitudes that shape how they perceive and experience life moment by moment.

This is unfortunate as these deeper patterns limit transformational growth and the development of more subtle enlightened states of awareness.

Therefore, self-understanding and insight into yourself when rightly used, is really a key component to unlocking your spiritual potential.

Your deeper spiritual essence and your Heart will only unfold to the degree that you are successful in working though the Mind, Body, Heart-Spirit patterns that are obstructing greater Truth and Self-Realization from being revealed.

If you are unaware of your personality patterns, your ego patterns and even how the ego itself is structured, then you will be unable to bring a deeper concentration and focus to discover their existence and how they literally run your life.

This process of self-discovery and spiritual transformation is fueled by insight. It is fueled by understanding how you are limiting your own presence from manifesting in each and every moment.

When you are able to go deeper and be more focused on your self-limiting patterns, you will begin to have a multitude of insights into those aspects of yourself that keep you "asleep", stressed and limited.

Then, through the spiritual wisdom and understanding that arises you can begin to shift and transform those patterns from a place of clarity. Consider that insight and self-understanding are like a beautiful eagle soaring high in the sky that has a clear overview of everything beneath it.

When a pattern begins to shift, Consciousness, which is the foundational energy that lies beneath the pattern, can begin to flow and expand thus increasing the experience of unity, presence and love.

If this deep work is not done, the energy stays locked up. It is the same as having valuables locked in a box. Even though they may be safe inside the box, they can't be enjoyed.

When the energy of Consciousness is locked up by your limiting patterns, your ability to evolve and transform is greatly reduced. Therefore the process of insight is a critical bridge in the journey of spiritual awakening. It is a process of inner self-discovery.

Once you begin this process, you then have to be willing to take what you discover and begin to transform it.

The first step is becoming aware of an aspect of yourself that is limiting your further development. Once you become aware of a limiting pattern you then have to feel deeply into it. You have to actually connect with it and feel the quality of the energy that is there.

Simply be present with whatever the energy is in a non-judgmental way, until you can relax into it and feel the energy expand. It is important that you feel a sense of inner space coexistent with the issue, as this shows an opening and relaxation is occurring. When this happens further insights about it will naturally arise in your awareness.

Then you must apply wisdom and insight to realign the pattern and if necessary, transform it. Transforming a pattern means changing it so that it supports your transformation rather than obstructs it.

It means that you now experience greater love, peace and harmony in relation to that pattern which previously created inner disturbance and disharmony.

Many patterns we have interfere with this process of inner transformation. They don't allow for greater self-discovery to take place. Rather than be a victim to these self-limiting patterns it is up to each one of us to do something about them.

Life itself is an ever changing dynamic process. Therefore, as much as we would like to think that once we get through a few tough challenges then everything will be smooth sailing, this is rarely the case.

Life is an ongoing process of growth and development that requires a profound level of insight and understanding about what is required to continue on the path of personal transformation.

Transformation is a multidimensional process. You have to stay focused and present in each moment in order to maximize inner and outer development.

Each moment of focus, awareness and self-observation, will open doorways leading to greater insight and knowledge about yourself and your spiritual journey. Then what is discovered can be applied to your life so that you can transform and evolve even further.

It is important to be aware that once you apply any significant changes to yourself and to your life, it will create a ripple effect throughout all facets and dimensions of your life. This will bring other things to your awareness that need to be explored, examined and questioned further.

Life is a continuous process of adaptation and change which requires wisdom and insight in order to be effective at a core level. Step by step you bring your life into greater alignment and harmony with the more aware, sensitive, awakened, enlightened you that lies beneath the patterns and stress.

Many people have the belief and hope that someone other than themselves will save them. Believers think that they can just pray to Jesus, Buddha or Mohammed to save them from their unhappy life and their dysfunctional life patterns.

To expect that your salvation is going to come through someone else is a huge dis-empowerment to your own authentic spiritual growth and transformation.

Do not look for a spiritual figure, guru or teacher to liberate you. They can be of great assistance but you must do the inner work that will lead to lasting and permanent transformation.

Thinking someone will do it for you is akin to looking for a magic pill to solve all the problems and challenges in life. In actuality, each pattern, belief and emotional feeling is very complex and subtle in its energy make up and may require a great deal of persistence and insight to be transformed.

No individual, aside from you, can take the time and effort that is required to bring about your inner transformation.

The next thing to realize is that that transformation requires regular focus and practice over time. If you are living your life and you notice that your attention is mostly absorbed with life issues – dealing with day to day issues of money, job, and relationship – then you are probably doing very little work on your self-limiting patterns.

It is not to say that those other things are not important but if they end up absorbing the majority of your focus, then there is usually little time left over for self-discovery and transformation.

This is why self-understanding and insight are so critical. They open the doors of wisdom that allow your Heart and awareness to expand into deeper and more subtle dimensions. This allows for greater transformation and awakening.

Many people think that wisdom has to do with the mind and intellect. However, there is a huge difference between deep Heart Wisdom and simply learning and memorizing something.

Most people function from memory rather than from wisdom. Wisdom requires you to be present and connected with the center of your Heart. Awakened Heart Wisdom is generated from inner observation and Heart felt feeling.

This is a very important distinction. As you unfold your spiritual journey you need to be aware of whether you are just thinking in your mind and using memory and intellect or whether you are freely observing with Heartfelt feeling into the present moment.

Also, there should to be moments of space between your observations and your feelings.

If you notice how the mind normally operates you will see that it is very, very busy. It goes from the one thought to the next and in that process of constant thinking, there is very little awareness of anything but the thoughts.

This lack of awareness makes it impossible to develop any depth of insight.

This is important because if you are not developing depth of insight then you are fundamentally unable to transform and like a broken record you just keep repeating the same life experiences over and over.

Thus it is critical to your journey to take mini insight, awareness and exploration breaks in order to open up a sense of internal space. Even if you take 10 minutes 2 or 3 times a day to sit, be silent and aware, you are creating the space for transformation to occur.

This inner space gives you a rest from your ego identity. It allows you to take a break from being constantly caught up in thinking, automatic behavior, effort and "doing" which is always stress producing and limiting.

As long as you stay engaged and busy it is unlikely that the deeper dimension of your awareness, your inner wisdom, will have an opportunity to shine through.

To get in touch with your inner being requires you to be aware of your life patterns and how they strangle the life force energy and prevent further evolution.

Bring a greater awareness to how your life is structured. Is it structured to allow for insight and balance or are you living the same way day after day, year after year?

If you are not maximizing and utilizing your life and the inherent potential that lays deep within for spiritual self-realization and human fulfillment, then it is a life that is not fully lived. You have not managed to unfold your true human spiritual potential.

When you begin to reflect on your journey and how to unfold your deeper dimensions, it is important to have an intention to bring a laser like focus and awareness to each arising moment.

If you do that, those deeper issues that relate to your life, whether they have to do with your relationships, work, the health of your body etc., can be transformed.

Insight is required to bring these different facets of yourself back into alignment. Then step by step your life as a whole can be harmonized and re-structured for your greatest transformation.

As you harmonize and align these parts of your life, more energy is freed up, more space is created, and greater awareness arises. It is a natural progression. It is very much like a snowball rolling down a hill that starts off slowly but builds momentum and strength as it continues its journey down the mountain.

Life is an ongoing process of unfolding your spiritual destiny. It is not just about unfolding your human life; it is really about unfolding who you are as eternal spiritual consciousness.

Self-understanding is an important ingredient to your overall development as an unfolding spiritual being. It leads to insight and to positive change in your life patterns.

Such things as meditation, yoga, eating a conscious diet and so forth, are important because we are multidimensional beings. It is incredibly helpful in our spiritual quest to align these various aspects of ourselves so that we may reach our full potential.

We are not just Consciousness; we are Consciousness in a human body that has emotions, thoughts, feelings and subtler dimensions beyond that. Therefore life becomes a process of awakening and aligning all these different dimensions of who we are.

There is no one technique, system or method that can address these multidimensional levels of who you are as a spiritual being.

The connecting link to transforming your being on every level is insight and understanding combined with Heart centered feeling and whole body awareness.

For example if you are eating a certain type of food you need to have an awareness and understanding of how that food is affecting your body. Does the food make you feel stronger, more centered, more balanced, or does it have a negative effect, causing stress and tension in your body?

If you are unconsciously eating then you are not aware enough to discover how the food that you are eating is affecting your life and the chance for insight and self-discovery that leads to Wisdom is lost.

It is the same thing with your emotional experience. Many people do not bring a deeper awareness to what they are feeling emotionally and energetically.

Most people in our society become so busy that they do not allow themselves the time and space to experience and therefore process their emotions and feelings. This is very detrimental because it creates a huge backlog of unprocessed unexpressed feelings and emotions that become an inner toxic stew.

If you are not currently experiencing your emotions and the feelings that go with them to any depth, you will not know if something is harmonious or disharmonious on a deeper energetic level.

If those emotional feelings are about a relationship for example, then you have to take the feelings and look firstly at the patterns within yourself and then at the patterns within the other person. Once you have done this it may be possible to have insight into how you can make the relationship deeper stronger and more harmonious.

Likewise you need to bring insight and understanding to your mental patterns and beliefs. Do your belief systems allow you to flow and be present in each moment? Or are your belief systems running interference patterns to the present moment?

Limiting belief patterns can only be transformed if you have insight and understanding into how they are affecting your experience as well as how they are affecting the unfolding of your spiritual awareness and energy.

This is important because the whole point of a human life is to unfold greater spiritual potential. However it just doesn't happen by itself. It requires an active focus on the part of each individual.

Once you bring a greater focus and awareness to the present moment, the answers and solutions you seek in your life will begin to reveal themselves within your conscious mind.

I strongly encourage each one of you to do this. If you do so you will progressively unfold and develop understanding and insight.

This is important for your life in general and for uncovering the limitations that may be holding back a beautiful flowering within the depths of your Heart.

Keep cultivating more Presence and Awareness and take one step after the other.

Eventually through your conscious aware choices, you will arrive at a more profound experience of who you have always been.

CHAPTER ELEVEN

Love is Forever but the Body is Not

Let us begin this consideration with the truth since that is always the best place to start. "Love is Forever" is a truthful statement of reality itself. Each of us, as a conscious being of light, presence and energy, is ultimately the expression of love. The expression of love that we each are is "forever" because we are eternal beings.

Therefore, this love has no beginning and it has no end. It is infinite, limitless, forever free and unconditioned by any of life's experiences. The real essence of the human journey is to awaken to this love and to unfold it progressively so that it can become a living reality.

The Awakened Heart is a heart that is in contact with, and is aware and cognizant of, this infinite love. In order to get back to this space of love, each human being has to go through a process of transformation and awakening.

From birth, we are conditioned into the experience that love is limited and finite in some way and that love comes from "another". We believe that we can only have love in relationship to another or when we are in love with something we do in our life.

People have their favorite hobby that they "love doing" or they feel love within an intimate relationship with their partner. Thus, we get used to the experience of love that is conditional and do not allow ourselves the opportunity to access the love that is forever.

There is nothing wrong with conditional love and it is certainly a beautiful part of the human journey however, the love that we share is just a doorway to the deeper love which is eternal.

We are used to the dualistic conditioned experience of love. This is where you either receive love from another or give love back to another.

This not only occurs between people. Many people absolutely love their pets. Some people actually love their pets more than they do people.

Whatever the object of your love is, the love that you feel is meant to be a doorway rather than a limitation, or something you become dependent upon and attached to. The reality is that the other person, your beloved pet, and things that you love will eventually die and fade away.

Everything in terms of the human life experience is finite. This is what I mean by Love is forever, but the body is not.

To move beyond the limitations of physical reality and our conditioning, we need to open and live through our Heart. This means we attempt to touch the love that is there in each moment and to recognize that we exist as that love.

Once you are living the experience of eternal love, there is no underlying fear or anxiety to any experience, including your own death or the death your loved ones.

Love is Forever but the Body is Not

In an intimate relationship, if we believe that love is dependent on the relationship that we are having, there is always an underlying anxiety. There is a deep fear that the love you are experiencing with the other person, could disappear.

The truth is that ultimately all forms, things, objects and people disappear. Yet interestingly, being able to experience love with another is a necessary stage in the unfolding of The Awakened Heart.

It is important to be able to open your Heart and be vulnerable. Most of us have been hurt at some point in the past. Many people have been emotionally traumatized or feel their heart has been unfairly hurt or rejected by family, friends and co-workers as well as by their intimate partner.

There are often divisions in families even where there is a close bond. The probability of emotional wounding is high and is most often caused by what someone says, does or omits to do.

Even parents getting divorced and going their separate ways can deeply traumatize the young children in the family. There are many ways a Heart can be wounded.

Underneath any experience of love that you have with another human being, there is simultaneously anxiety, fear, and tension. On an unconscious level, we believe love is to be found outside ourselves in "another", and therefore that love can be "lost".

The ego, which develops as you grow and mature, creates your identity as a separate human being.

As that process occurs, you become progressively desensitized to the deeper dimensions of the Heart and begin to live more and more from thoughts, concepts, and beliefs.

It is inevitable therefore that you will experience love in a limited, conditional way. However, the reality is that love is forever. Therefore, as you unfold your spiritual journey you have to go through a radical metamorphosis of what you feel and believe about love and about life itself.

It is not sufficient to feel love in moments with certain people or certain situations in life. There needs to be a deeper impulse in you that wants to discover the very Essence of Love itself. An impulse that leads you to embrace the essence of love that is always there deep within your own Heart.

However, most people cannot experience this love that is forever because they are in lost in patterns of reaction, contraction and stress.

These negative life patterns act like a glove that is worn over the exquisite silkiness of our Heart. Because the glove is there, we can no longer feel the beautiful texture of our Heart's subtle energy, which is made of love, peace and joy.

Since we are unable to feel that deep love, we believe that love must come from the outside and not from within us. Therefore we form this inner conviction that love itself is only available in limited and conditional circumstance in life.

As you evolve and progressively remove that glove from your Heart you begin to sense and feel the subtlety of love. Then overtime it may suddenly start to dawn on you that Love is not limited and conditional.

Love is Forever but the Body is Not

From that point onwards, you become more and more centered in that energy of love and can directly experience for yourself, beyond mental concepts, that Love is forever. This experience dissolves the fear and anxiety that was the undercurrent of your life prior to this point.

This is not a love that can be taken away. Eventually your being awakens to this Truth of Existence. Each of us has to work through the various fears and issues that we have that prevent us from experiencing and knowing this deeper Truth of Reality directly prior to mental interpretations.

Therefore, our focus needs to be on uncovering what is obstructing the experience of the love that is forever. Touching on and feeling that eternal love profoundly changes your experience as a human being.

It deeply changes how you perceive life as well as your behavior and life choices. We become a living, radiant, demonstration of love itself as we unfold year after year in this human form.

The essence of the love that is forever does not have to say anything. Like the sun, it simply radiates its presence and its life supporting warmth to all and everything.

There are many ways that you can help the people that you love. However, the greatest way you can help is by sharing the love that is forever. By simply being anchored and aware of this Divine Love deep within your Heart, you are transforming the world around you.

When you share this love, you are bringing a divine light and energy into the present moment and to the planet which for the most part is de-void of love.

A large part of humanity is asleep in relation to this love and many people are actually afraid of it. You can see this in our history. Why was Christ crucified? He died because he represented something radically different from what was acceptable to the people in power and to people in general, at that time.

Many people fear the power of spiritual love. For them it is frightening because they have not yet begun to undertake the deeper journey of healing the various aspects their own Heart. They have not begun to release the pain that is there which would allow an awakening to their spiritual essence fueled by the energetic radiance of real love.

Understanding all of this to be true mentally and intellectually is not enough. If insight and wisdom are not infused with the essence of an Awakened Heart, then the experience of love will not last. It will not be an experience that will be forever.

As you awaken to your spiritual Heart, you will awaken to the greater potential of who you are. Then, with intention, passion and focus you can bring this into manifestation.

It is not an easy process. If it were easy, everybody would be radiating the essence of love and life on the planet would be harmonious and beautiful.

Consider your life and look at how challenging it is to be loving in each moment in the face of a world that is unconscious and deeply pained. It takes great courage and intention for any individual to awaken.

It will not simply just happen by itself. There is a saying in the Bible that goes something to the effect, "Love the Lord thy God with all your heart and soul".

Even that statement needs to be refined. The real essence of that statement is, make love your first priority so that you awaken to the Divine love within yourself, which is God or Consciousness.

If you make love the first priority in your life, you can be assured that you are walking a path that is the most balanced and harmonious for yourself and for others.

By making love, your first intention you are serving your own highest good, the highest good of all the souls that you love, and that of the collective community as well.

So make love your first focus in life. If you do so, the inner radiance and presence that is contained within your Heart will progressively get stronger.

Instead of putting one foot in front of the other stay focused on the next heartbeat. Focus on one heartbeat after another and do your best to discover what the core energy and essence is, that keeps your Heart beating for a lifetime.

You will discover over time that this essence is eternal, infinite love.

This love dissolves all fear and anxiety leaving only a deep inner peace and contentment that is beyond words. Awaken to the Love that is Forever and Reality will happily greet and embrace you with arms that reach out to infinity.

CHAPTER TWELVE

Unfolding the Experience of Unity and
Overcoming the Conviction of Separateness

We will begin this discussion by looking at the way in which most human beings experience themselves moment to moment and day by day.

At the core of most people's daily experience, is the experience of separateness.

They live their life as if they are separate from other people and things, and separate from the Reality of themselves as eternal conscious spiritual beings.

At the root of every human being's unhappiness is this experience of separateness.

If the sense of separateness did not exist, there would not be the pain, suffering and disillusionment that so many people experience in life. All of the anxiety, stress and tension and would no longer exist as we currently know and experience it.

When the experience of separateness is absent, you can be absolutely present in every moment. From this relaxed aware Presence comes a natural flow and harmony with people, things and with life itself.

When you are able to be present, the essence of who you are as Consciousness becomes immediately available to you. This energy becomes the source from which you live your life.

When you live from this energy, there is no dilemma or any sense of underlying anxiety permeating your day to day existence. You then have the capacity to live as a free, aware, loving soul who continues evolving and transforming within the context of ordinary human life.

Resolving the inner experience of separateness is one of the critical aspects of the human spiritual journey. Since this is such a vital part of the spiritual journey, why is it that most of us never move beyond this experience?

The core experience of separateness is fundamentally ignored and denied, as well as unconsciously repressed by most people. This deep unquestioned experience of separation is at the Heart of everyone's suffering yet no one even seems to be aware of it. How bizarre is that?

When people live life based on a core belief of separateness, they experience separateness as real.

Yet many enlightened beings and mystics from various paths and spiritual traditions agree that the experience of separateness is not one that is based in Reality.

For most people however, whether separateness is in fact real, is something that remains unexamined within their own immediate experience.

This unquestioned acceptance permeates everyone's life and influences their perception and every experience they are having.

You really have to go back to the process of birth and development from infant to teenager, to understand that the experience of separateness is not arising from just a thought.

It is not just a belief, it is actually an experience. Thinking is just an external layer. What is at the core of this belief structure is an actual experience of separateness. Thought simply reinforces experience.

When you are a small infant, you come out of the experience of unity and wholeness into the world of form. As you do so, your nervous system begins to develop which allows you to eventually function as an independent human being.

From this point, you begin to develop an awareness of the body as distinct from other things.

The nerves and cells of the brain, the nervous system, the meridian channels and the energy centers, all develop in a way that informs your brain that you are indeed a separate entity.

The physical body defines itself as separate from other bodies and separate from the environment.

This belief/experience of separateness exists at the core of your unconscious mind and is the foundation stone of your moment to moment experience.

As you continue to grow and develop, your mind and belief systems form based upon the experience of separateness.

The culture you live in determines the language you learn, your beliefs, and your religious practices, until you grow old enough to make your own decisions.

Underlying this whole process of conditioning is a nervous system that is immersed in the experience of separateness. Your brain, your nervous system and senses all inform you that you are a separate entity.

We know from scientific studies that our senses are in fact very limited and that many animals can see, hear and smell much better than we can yet we rarely question the results our senses provide us.

Even less do we question the experience of separateness – we accept it as the only reality.

The irony or the cosmic joke is that the experience we are having as a separate self is not one based in Reality. It is actually just a conditioned experience.

Spiritual traditions talk about reality as "unconditional". They describe reality as the experience of unconditional love, unlimited happiness, infinite peace, and limitless bliss.

Our soul essence is fundamentally unlimited and free, yet at the core of our human experience is the conviction that the experience of being a person, who is separate from all other beings, is reality.

This has huge ramifications because you are then making choices in life, based on this deep inner conviction.

Therefore everything you do, your behavior, what interests you, how you live your life, the relationships that you have, and the entire gamut of your existence is being lived from this viewpoint of separateness.

This is why various spiritual traditions and enlightened beings say that eventually you have to transcend the experience of separateness.

In order to do that and to change this deep inner conviction of separateness, you have to have a direct experience that transcends the experience of separateness itself.

This deeply engrained conviction of separateness makes up the very fabric of your cells and your nervous system so it is extremely difficult to shift. This is why it is so challenging for human beings to Wake Up!

It is impossible to know and experience who you truly are as long as you are living your life from the experiential viewpoint separateness.

This is where wisdom, insight, and understanding of the human spiritual journey, is critical.

Let's say you have some life issues, perhaps self-worth issues, emotional issues, anger issues etc., issues that are limiting you from experiencing greater love and happiness in your life.

There are self-help programs, ego self-improvement practices and positive thinking practices; however all these things are remedial at best.

There is a big confusion in the New Age Movement and even in most religions and spiritual paths regarding self-improvement methods and systems.

Many of these will help you to feel better within the experience of separateness, but are not in and of themselves designed to move you beyond the experience of separateness.

For example, it is quite common today in the west for people to practice yoga.

However, most people are practicing yoga from the viewpoint of releasing tension, getting a little more relaxed, or just feeling a little better about themselves.

There is nothing wrong with any of that except that the people doing the practice, still experience themselves as a separate being/person.

These types of practices do not assist in releasing the core structure and belief of separateness. Only when the experience of separateness is transcended is it possible to bring about a permanent state of truthful Presence and awareness, also referred to as Enlightenment.

Even if you embrace spiritual practices and are meditating, doing energy practices etc. as a "separate self", then you are once again, caught up in self-improvement practices that remain rooted in the experience of separateness.

No matter how much self-improvement work you do, if you do not transcend the core experience of separation, none of it will awaken you. It will not transcend the deep dilemma and anxiety that rises from separateness.

The most important and significant event that can occur within an individual's life is to have an experience that takes them beyond separateness into unity.

For example, people who go through a near death experience usually return to their bodies with a completely different perception of reality. Reports from people who have had this experience have many common features.

They say they could feel their soul separating out from their body, followed usually by visual experiences of going into a tunnel of light and energy. Then once in the tunnel they experienced feelings of love, joy, unity and presence.

After a period of time, they could feel themselves come back into their body again. From that point onwards, their perception of life and reality is fundamentally altered.

They are no longer convinced that they are merely a separate body. Many of them completely change the way they relate to the world because of this shift in their inner experience.

To be clear, I am not saying that the experience that you are having in the body is an illusion, what I am saying is that it is not the full picture. It is a partial experience, not the full infinite, unconditioned experience of reality as it really is.

Many spiritual systems and paths approach the "cure" for separateness by trying to transcend the body. They focus on going beyond it by taking up various meditation practices oriented towards ascension.

Actually, there is nothing to "get rid of" and no need to ascend anywhere. What you have to transcend, is the experience of separateness.

If you remove the experience of separateness there is no problem, no dilemma, nowhere to go and everything in you falls into a harmonious alignment with what "Is" which is Awareness, Consciousness and Presence.

There are beings that for some inexplicable reason have spontaneously awakened beyond the experience of separateness, to experience pure consciousness and presence. Eckhart Tolle is an example of this, but it is exceptionally rare.

Some people who have embraced the spiritual path, who meditate and who practice harmonizing and balancing their life also reach this experience of Unity that transcends the experience of separateness.

However you are talking about maybe less than one percent of people who are living "A spiritual life".

Others have a very pure intention but despite that, may not ever overcome the inner conviction of separateness.

Another trap for people on the spiritual path is the belief that being on a "path" or doing "spiritual practices" will make them enlightened or at least better human beings.

This is not necessarily so for if the person practicing the path is still in the core experience of separateness then being on a "path" can become just another ego trip.

The personal ego patterns easily transfer over to being a "spiritual person" who is now somehow better than other people.

You might feel better in your body, you might feel a little more harmonious and it might make your overall life experience more positive, but it does not guarantee that you will permanently transcend your experience of separateness.

A traditional path, which is quite common in many native cultures over the last few thousand years, is the shamanic path or passage of initiation and ritual.

Many of these cultures included native plants that would alter people's state of consciousness.

This was the traditional way of giving someone the experience of going beyond the limited sense of separateness to directly experience the spirit world.

Another traditional approach is receiving energy transmission from an Awakened Teacher who is already in the experience and awareness of Unity. This is based on the principle of one candle being able to light another.

Bottom line, it is very difficult to awaken one's Heart from the crushing experience of separateness.

That is why most people live from this core experience from the moment they are born until their last breath.

Remember as you grow into adulthood, the mind simply reinforces the experience of separateness in the nervous system and the body.

Therefore, unless you have an experience that awakens you or sets you on a course that leads you to the truth beyond this conviction then to put it rather bluntly, you are condemned to a life of separateness.

What you can do right now as a first step to overcoming this limited experience of separateness is to contemplate the discussion we are sharing in this present moment.

Deeply consider this core conviction of separateness so that you begin to loosen your automatic unconscious behavior and perceptions of life.

With great tenacity and sincerity begin to question your life experience which is based on this experience of separateness.

If you do not question the experience you are having and the point of view from which you live your life, there is unlikely to be any significant change.

Unless there is a dramatic event or a spontaneous awakening, you will continue to live a life based on separateness rather than experiencing Unity which is your true nature.

This is where the Awakened Heart Path comes into the equation. Ultimately, it is through the Heart that you will dissolve the experience of separateness.

The Heart is a deeply feeling sensitive organ and registers the sense of separateness. This is why the Heart is the most critical component to the whole transcendence of separation and awakening to unity.

So keep bringing your focus to the Heart and notice how you are feeling in each moment. Notice the sense of separateness and question that experience.

Keep your focus in the Heart and on the body and begin to question your behaviors, especially those that are automatic and habitual. With persistent focus and practice they will gradually shift and dissolve over time.

Thus, the core to unfolding Unity is to focus on the Heart and to question the experience of separateness.

This is not just a mental exercise, although in this process your beliefs will change. It is about changing an actual experience that you have come to believe is real.

If you do not change the experience of separateness, in the core of your Heart, then all the positive thinking you practice and all the spiritual beliefs you have will not amount to anything of significance.

Many spiritual paths and churches give sermons and talks about being One with the Divine, but how many people within those systems are actually living the experience of Unity on a permanent basis?

The most important thing is to begin to Live the practice of being One, which you do from your Heart.

As your Heart awakens, it progressively softens and begins to dissolve the barriers that prevent a free flow of subtle energy from the Heart to your entire physical energetic system.

The Heart creates the electromagnetic field of the body. It also directly affects the nervous system and the neurons in the brain that hold your beliefs of separateness in words, images and belief constructs.

As you begin to change the vibration of the Heart by clearing away the barriers, it automatically starts to shift the nervous system and your entire experience. Therefore, this is the place to put your focus and your intention.

If you have a deep commitment to experience who you truly are, which is oneness, unity, infinite love, peace, and freedom then you can do something to make it a living, authentic experience in your life.

It takes wisdom, great insight and understanding as well as the ongoing practice of living as One from the Heart.

If you can do this, gradually you will awaken and unfold in your own unique way. What a grand and beautiful thing that will be.

CHAPTER THIRTEEN

The Spiritual Teacher and Mentor

The next step in our exploration of the Awakened Heart Path and our human potential is to discuss the importance of the Spiritual Teacher.

If we set out on a journey with a destination in mind, we generally consult a map or these days, our GPS.

The idea being that you need directions or some sort of reference, to know where you are going. You need to know if you are getting closer to your goal or going in the wrong direction.

On the spiritual journey, the Spiritual Teacher is potentially your best friend, supporter, and ally as your path unfolds over your lifetime.

The Teacher is someone who can give you truthful and insightful guidance and input that will assist you in addressing the challenges and difficulties that lie ahead of you.

Ultimately the unfolding of your journey and your potential, is always up to you...it is your choice and your decision alone to make. However if you are truly sincere and would like assistance and guidance then the Teacher is there to help you.

In the human spiritual journey, there are many pitfalls and many potential dark alleys that can swallow you up body, mind, and soul.

These are the areas of the unconscious which include not only thoughts and beliefs but also past emotional traumas and emotional energy that become stuck in the physical and subtle energy bodies.

These dimensions of yourself must be brought into the light of awareness so that they are "enlightened" and therefore transformed. Then your whole being can come into alignment with truthful reality.

One important facet of the Teacher's work is to help the student become aware of any aspects of themselves of which they are unconscious. For that which you remain unaware of, you cannot transform and address.

The greatest limitations are the ones that cannot be seen by the individual due to the way in which the ego functions.

The spiritual life process, the human process, is about uncovering that which is unconscious and bringing it to light. It is about evolution and evolution is a process of progressive revelation and transformation.

The Spiritual Teacher helps you overcome this tricky part of the journey and reduces the likelihood that you will become stuck in the multitude of self-limiting ego patterns that we all have.

Then who you truly are as Spiritual Being can actually become a living experience rather than something you just believe in or read about in a book.

It is really about uncovering the bliss that is already within you and the Love that you already are. All of that is always right here, right Now.

First and foremost the Spiritual Teacher is there to help you to Wake Up. The Spiritual Teacher can at times be very annoying and disturbing to the Ego and its patterns of limitation.

The Teacher is annoying to the ego because the ego wants to stay asleep. Thus there are times when you will not appreciate the Teacher who is there to help move you beyond your ego structure.

It is this ego structure that is at the root of your suffering and unless you sincerely desire transformation you will resist mightily anything the Teacher may point out to you.

However, the good news is that part of you does want to wake up and would like assistance to move beyond the ego and its process of limitation. It is inherent in each of our souls to want freedom from the constraints of limited ego identity.

Each of us at a core level wants to be fulfilled and wants to experience what it is like to be absolutely peaceful, present and fulfilled.

We have a deep inner longing to experience union and a state of oneness. It is imprinted deep within the DNA of each of our souls.

Yes, it is comfortable when you are deeply asleep, it is a really peaceful space to be, but at some point, you have to wake up. It is possible to travel for lifetimes and be unaware that your True Nature is infinite light, bliss and love.

The Spiritual Teacher is needed most, when you begin that awakening process.

The Teacher functions not only as a wisdom guide, but also as someone who becomes acquainted with you on a very deep and intimate level as they are aware of dimensions that you have not yet awoken to.

They can assist you by creating an energetic environment of unconditional love and acceptance of who you are and by showing you where you are heading on your journey.

When you feel unconditional love and acceptance you begin to relax and accept yourself and your journey. This is, obviously, a big part of the spiritual journey.

Accepting where you are at, what you are experiencing and bringing a greater awareness to it, is a significant part to one's spiritual development.

This happens most effectively when you are able to be Present. Another key function of the Teacher is to assist you in simply becoming Present, to be right here, right now.

Having a Teacher who can assist you to bring your mind and all inner activity to a place of stillness where Presence and Awareness can directly emerge for you, is extremely important.

The Teacher, having traveled down the same spiritual path you are on, knows from first-hand experience what lays ahead of you and what will assist you on your journey.

If you are the adventurous type of spiritual seeker, you may want to head out and blaze a trail into the unknown on your own.

However exceptionally few beings have the capacity to change from a state of unconscious sleep to a state of being awake, whole and complete, on their own.

Therefore, it makes much more sense to have a Teacher who can guide you and explain the process that you will be going through.

Another important function of the Teacher is they demonstrate that you can go into the unconscious, the "dark night of the soul", and come out the other side with your sanity still intact. At times spiritual transformation of one's ego patterns can be terrifying to put it mildly.

To know that there is someone in your life who has gone through the unraveling process of the ego can be extremely comforting.

In general though, our egos and personal identities do not want to be unraveled and dissolved. Just think of who you are right now and your whole life history. The ego does not want that to disappear into the infinite sea of Reality. This is the "Catch 22".

To awaken is to actualize your human spiritual potential, and to live from that infinite eternal state of loving presence and awareness.

However, in order to awaken you have to uncover, clear and remove the obstacles and the obstructions that do not allow your inner radiance to shine.

The ego is not necessarily interested in that process.

Thus, there is a push-pull dichotomy in effect. Deep down every soul wants to be happy and wants to experience Love. Simultaneous to this deep wish is the obstructing dynamic of the ego that wants to keep everything the same.

There is a part of us that would just like to live forever the way we are, unless life becomes such a suffering that we are forced to make a change.

To continue to grow spiritually, you have to let go, you have to surrender and overcome the inertia that the ego creates.

To illustrate this, consider the analogy of a river flowing to the ocean, the ocean being a representation of the infinite nature of consciousness.

The river is like your ego identity; it is contained within a small area between two banks and can be seen and known. It is made of the same material as the ocean but stays small and limited, confined by its banks.

So much of the time, we want to stay comfortable by remaining safe within the boundaries of the riverbanks. We want to cling to what we know and to what is familiar so that we feel in control.

However, like the river, our ultimate goal is to reach the spiritual ocean and expand into its vast space.

In order to do that, we have to let go.

This is why so many spiritual paths emphasize, "letting go" or surrender. When people think of the word of surrender, they tend to think of it as surrender to something else or to someone outside of themselves.

If something happens in your life, either you can fight it, or you can surrender to it. The same thing applies to your spiritual journey.

You can either fight that process of awakening or surrender to it and allow yourself to be taken by the flow of the river, to the ocean.

The Teacher is there to guide you in this process of letting go of the seeming safety of your ego identity so that you can continue flowing down the river of life to the spiritual ocean that awaits you.

While you are still asleep, the Teacher appears in the form of a separate being whose task is to give you guidance and direction. You relate to the Teacher as another separate being.

However, the Teacher sees you as he sees himself and that is simply as a spiritual being whose nature is divine love and Consciousness. The Teacher does not experience you as separate from himself but rather as another expression of eternal energy.

If you are working with a Spiritual Teacher it is important to be aware of any internal resistance. Where there is resistance you will hinder the Teacher's ability to be of assistance to you both on a spiritual wisdom level as well as a transformational energetic level.

Again this is the nature of the ego which wants to resist change.

Therefore, what is required in the process of awakening is that the individual be willing and open to take instruction and guidance, with an attitude of appreciation and trust.

An essential part of the journey is based on the principle of letting go and surrendering and in order to do that you have to have both faith and trust in the Teacher and more importantly in yourself.

As you open and move forward in your journey, the Teacher is there to guide you each step of the way as well as provide encouragement.

The Teacher encourages you to keep going and to never give up no matter what you may face or how difficult the journey may become.

The Teacher knows how important it is to keep going and not become stuck in any experience good or bad. The Teacher is not someone who is going to force you to make changes in your life; he/she will simply invite you to make those changes for yourself based on your own inner desire and passion for transformation.

THE ENERGETIC PHYSICS OF SPIRITUAL TRANSFORMATION

Another significant role that the Teacher plays is that of Energetic Transformer. The Teacher having cleared and released many obstacles and blockage within their own energetic system and structure becomes a conduit and channel for the subtle life force energy of Consciousness.

This is also referred to as Presence. The more present the Teacher the greater the flow of life force and the greater potential transformation that the individual seeker and student can experience.

When the individual surrenders their internal resistance there is an opening within them that allows for Enlightening Presence, Energy and Awareness to enter.

It is this energy of Consciousness along with the individual's intention and focus that brings about a direct and efficient Awakening. Thus, the Spiritual Teacher is an energy source of Enlightening Presence.

This Presence allows the person to expand their awareness and to gain insight into their self-limiting patterns. In this way, they can see and discover what is blocking Presence from manifesting directly within their own life.

There is much more to life than waking up each morning and having a good relationship and a great job. Ultimately, there is a much greater process taking place than just the day-to-day life experience and that process involves this mostly untapped and hidden spiritual dimension.

The whole point of engaging in the process of awakening is so that you can fully enjoy your life. It is not about giving up and reducing your life to nothing or living some austere or ascetic life.

Spiritual awakening is really about creating your life in such a way that you can live it with full joy and happiness. The Spiritual Teacher is there to facilitate this process within an individual.

The commitment to grow has to come from within you. Then the guided assistance can flow into the space that this internal commitment to transformation, creates.

As much as you may want to unfold your life in an independent way, it is necessary to recognize that life is a co-creative process.

We may see ourselves as independent and separate but the ultimate reality is that there is a mutual interdependence.

The Authentic Teacher provides multi-dimensional, holistic, assistance and guidance to the spiritual seeker who is on a path of personal transformation.

Ultimately, the Spiritual Teacher and you are one, because truly, there is no such thing as separateness. The Teacher only appears as a separate being until you mature spiritually and recognize that Oneness within your own Heart.

CHAPTER FOURTEEN

Living in Harmony is Essential to Awakening the Heart

The focus of this chapter is living in harmony – an essential part of the journey to awakening and greater transformation.

Harmony is the principle of aligning your life in such a way that it has a natural flow to it. Harmony is essential to greater spiritual awakening and transformation for without it, your life is in a state of stress or "dis-ease".

As you grow and transform it is essential to look at each aspect of your life in relation to the principal of "harmony". This principle can be easily understood using the analogy of an orchestra.

An orchestra has many different components to it. Every instrument has a different range of sound and vibration and for the music to sound beautiful; each of the instruments within the orchestra has to play in harmony with all the others.

If they do not, the sound is chaotic and we feel stressed by the music rather than peaceful, happy and relaxed.

Each of us is really an orchestra, with many parts to our being. Thus our responsibility in life is to harmonize all the different components and facets that make up who we are, so that the music of consciousness can play freely through our form.

This principle applies to the physical, mental, emotional and spiritual levels of our being. However, if you are like most people you probably only focus on one or two dimensions of yourself while ignoring others.

Waking up is a Holistic process that requires great insight, intelligence, awareness and sensitivity to all facets of your being, many of which you may not be aware of at this current stage of your journey.

In essence, the journey is really quite simple: you just need to play a more beautiful song each day using your Heart as the conductor of your inner orchestra.

The spiritual journey is about cultivating a broad range of harmonious melodies that your whole being; Body, Mind and Heart-Spirit, can play.

The un-awakened personality-self always defines and limits the range of sounds and melodies that it can play. It also affects what and how you share and express with other souls in your world.

Overcoming these limiting tendencies, involves a process of introspection and insight into what is working in your inner and outer life. It also involves looking carefully at what is not working and is therefore blocking the creation and expression of greater harmony.

So much, of who we are as spiritual beings, remains dormant because we are not yet in harmony with the deeper parts of ourselves. There remain aspects of our being that function in an isolated way, rather than in rhythm with the totality of a unified whole.

If we want to create harmony in our life then there are two main dimensions for us to explore and consider. The first dimension concerns creating inner harmony.

Creating inner harmony involves bringing aspects of our mind, emotions and physical body into a state of flow and alignment. Much of the time, we go through life thinking and totally lost to the present moment because our minds usurp the majority of our focus and attention.

We get so absorbed in our thoughts that we lose touch with the emotional feeling dimension of ourselves. We do not feel the deeper dimensions of our Heart or even our entire body to any great degree. We become dis-connected from all the different parts that make up who we are.

Dis-connection is a state of "dis-ease" and minimal self-awareness.

It is important to remember that the Heart is the conductor of our personal inner orchestra. It directs and processes the details of our life. Therefore, it is very important to keep your Heart constantly in your awareness.

If you are totally absorbed in your thoughts: thinking about what you have to do today, what happened yesterday, or about what you are going to do tomorrow there is very little awareness left over to focus on your Heart and your feelings. This creates a state of disharmony.

If inner harmony is lacking there is very little possibility for transformation to occur. Very little real growth happens. The first step is always to be aware of whether you are experiencing harmony or dis-harmony within your current experience.

If holistic unfolding and spiritual evolution is what you value and what you would like to nurture in your life, then you need to give it the proper amount of time, energy and focus.

Cultivating inner harmony is a very important part of one's journey. We are aiming to create harmony between our thoughts, our feelings and of course our physical body.

This is what I refer to as the Sacred Trinity. The Sacred Trinity comprises your physical, emotional and mental dimensions.

The art of the spiritual journey is learning how to integrate these primary dimensions of the Sacred Trinity so that they work in unison and harmony.

This is something that takes deep sensitivity and insight into what is occurring within your being, moment to moment. Just as the conductor needs to be able to hear the music from the entire orchestra, you need to be able to hear, feel and sense the inner music of your Body, Mind and Heart-Spirit.

To conduct your inner orchestra takes energy because you are attempting to unify and weave together several dimensions (instruments) of yourself that are usually experienced as separate.

Living in Harmony is Essential to Awakening the Heart

As you begin to harmonize these different dimensions, the spiritual energy of Consciousness progressively shines through your entire being.

If there is internal disharmony, you are unable to benefit from the deeper more subtle spiritual energy. The loving presence of Consciousness cannot come through.

Because most people are in a state of disharmony, what they experience in life is a fairly constant state of stress and "dis-ease." Their inner orchestra is playing all kinds of funky, discordant notes and this is reflected in their experience of life.

As you develop the ability to stay connected to your inner self and to be present, which is a state of harmony, you are able to unfold in a holistic way. This is why the cornerstone of spiritual growth and transformation is based on developing and creating inner harmony.

Outer harmony however, is equally important. Our existence here on planet earth is greatly impacted by the environment that we live in, the relationships we have and the work that we do. Your outer life is equally important to your overall holistic growth and transformation.

For example, if you are in a relationship that is disharmonious, it will create stress in your life that will directly affect your inner experience. This can even be observed in your biochemistry. A simple blood test will reveal bio-chemical stress shown by the increase cortisol levels and other bio-chemicals in the body.

Thus it is important to create harmonious relationships in your life especially with your intimate partner, family, friends, workers and colleagues. The harmony that you create in your personal relationships will enhance and increase the overall level of harmony in your life.

There is a common expression that says: "If you want to experience more love in your life then be more loving". The same thing can be said for relationships. If you want to improve, your relationships begin by getting in touch with your Heart which is the Source of all Love.

Whatever you express within your current relationships, do your best in each moment to express from your Heart with sincerity and feeling. Keep the focus on your Heart and communicate what your truth is. It is very important to be aware of how your communication is affecting your Heart as well as the Heart of the other person.

This is not always an easy or pleasant process. Sometimes we have to express things that come from a deep inner wound that is a result of past trauma from other relationships. We always carry our trauma with us until we consciously deal with it. We carry our past with us and we bring our past into our current relationships.

However, we can use our current relationships as a tool to heal our wounds from the past by keeping our Heart open and seeing what arises for us to deal with.

Therefore, in your quest to cultivate outer harmony, it is vital to be aware of your relationships and to consider how you are living within those relationships.

Living in Harmony is Essential to Awakening the Heart

The places you find it difficult to create a loving flow and connection are where you need to look at the dynamics of your own inner process as well as the outer dynamics of the person that you are attempting to connect and commune with.

The next thing to consider when creating outer harmony is your environment. Are you living in an environment that is peaceful, beautiful and serene or one that is chaotic, fragmented and noisy?

If you consciously create a peaceful, loving environment then it automatically brings you greater tranquility.

Doing simple things such as cleaning your house, using essential oils, burning candles, putting flowers in your room, playing relaxing harmonious music are all ways to create an atmosphere of peace and tranquility.

How our modern society is structured and operates is a reflection of the total chaos that exists within most people and within our culture. Many people have the television or radio on most of the time or they are constantly talking on the phone or working on their computers. They have all kinds of "busyness" and activity happening within their environment that keeps them distracted and fragmented.

This kind of environment is not conducive to relaxation and harmony. Thus, it can be detrimental to the unfolding of your spiritual energy. It is important to take what I call "Harmony Breaks" throughout the day in order to maintain inner balance and harmony.

Another important area to consider is the work that you do. Do you enjoy what you are doing?

If you do not enjoy what you are doing in life, you are in a state of dis-ease and distress for many hours of the day. However, if you enjoy the work that you do it can be a great contribution to the creation of outer harmony.

If you are currently in a job that you do not love, create a plan that will allow you to align your life with the kind of work that is fulfilling for you. Always maintain the knowledge that if you don't like the way your life is now, you can change and transform it over time to be what you desire.

It takes time, patience and relentless persistence to create positive change in your life.

Obviously, there are some things that you cannot readily change in your outer world. However, if you take the time and energy to crystallize your intentions you can move systematically towards a more satisfying and harmonious future.

Take a moment here and now. Sit down and crystallize your thoughts about what you want from life. What do you want to do in life, where do you want to live, what kind of an environment would you like to be in and what sort of relationship would satisfy you?

When you clarify these questions you can progress towards your goals and develop greater harmony as your life unfolds. It all requires your active participation.

Living in Harmony is Essential to Awakening the Heart

As human beings, we have a tendency to stagnate and we often just passively accept our life situation.

This habit does not allow a person to create harmony in their life. If your current circumstances do not support the ever greater unfolding of your spiritual being, then some change is necessary.

The importance of creating outer harmony along with inner harmony cannot be overstated.

You can do yoga forever; you can meditate, work on your diet and do all the things that help to develop inner harmony. However, if you do not simultaneously take care of the outer part of your life, then there is still an inner fracture and misalignment within yourself and within your life creation.

No matter how well you may be doing on an internal level, if your outer world does not reflect that internal harmony, you will still experience limitation.

It is your birthright to experience the ultimate states of love, joy, peace and freedom. That is who you are as Consciousness, and who you are as Spirit. Whether people are aware of it or not, there is a deep desire within each person to create a loving and harmonious life.

We each long to experience and know who we are as spiritual beings, but this requires the principle of Harmony to be integrated into our daily life experience.

Whatever you do in life, try to do it with an awareness of harmony. If you do that, all the different facets that make up your inner and outer life can grow together. If you maintain this one focus and principal, you can make progress in many seemly divergent areas of your life.

Harmony is a very subtle and at times a difficult principle to bring into one's awareness. This is due to the fact that we do not consciously attempt to cultivate it in our lives.

Harmony encompasses such a huge range of our human existence, yet is something that most of us give very little focus or consideration to. We spend very little time even considering how to develop it.

The question is how can we create more harmony so that who we are as a spiritual being can progressively shine forth and be free? Once again, the essence of this comes back to the Heart, since the Heart is the director of the spiritual journey.

It is important to keep your Heart at the center of whatever you do in life. You can work on many different areas of yourself, both inner and outer. However, if the Heart is not at the center of it all, none of what you do will bring you into alignment with the principle of Harmony.

Due to the chaos of human existence, it is very easy to end up on a side road in the quest for wholeness and spiritual growth. Stay sensitized and aware of your Heart, otherwise the personality-self (your ego) will try to run the show.

The ego is like an instrument that decides to conduct its own little orchestra without being entirely aware of what the performance is about.

It is important to keep an ongoing awareness and consideration of Harmony or what I like to call Life Harmony.

Living in Harmony is Essential to Awakening the Heart

Remember Harmony is an energy-feeling-awareness, not a mental concept.

You know you are creating more Harmony in your life when there is a corresponding increase in your experience of love, joy and happiness.

It will allow your spirit to grow so that you feel your life is unfolding something of value. Of course that which has the greatest value, is your spiritual transformation. Nothing has more significance.

Everything else that we may look upon as having value will disappear. It will eventually be transformed into something else.

The physical body that you inhabit will disappear someday. However, the life you create generates the energy of Harmony or dis-harmony and that energy lives on long after the body dies.

Therefore, create Love and Harmony. They have to do with your soul's development in relation to the bigger picture of life. Then you can be sure that step by step, you will find greater peace and happiness.

The Heart is the true conductor and director of your life and is essential to unfolding this principle of harmony. If you allow your Heart to be your guide, you will be in tune with the great dance of Reality and oh what a dance that would be!

CHAPTER FIFTEEN

Heart Coherence...
The Merging of Science and Mysticism

Each of us understands that no man or woman is an island unto themselves. One of the main things we are attempting to discover in spiritual life is that we are all connected.

We are looking for the essential unity that lies beneath the seemingly individuated forms which inhabit our world. We seek to cultivate and expand this experience in all dimensions of our life.

This is where the Heart enters the equation. It is impossible to experience unity and oneness if you do not develop and cultivate the spiritual dimension of awareness that pertains to the Heart center.

Many spiritual traditions refer to the Heart as the seat of the soul. It is the center point from which everything in your being unfolds, grows and transforms. If you lose this center, life is full of chaos, confusion and delusion.

If you have lost your center you have lost awareness of what is ultimately real and true.

The heading of this chapter is "Heart Coherence: The Merging of Science and Mysticism". This is a very important and relevant topic for the times in which we live.

Heart coherence has to do with how the heart beats moment to moment. It refers to a heart rhythm that is in a state of harmony and balance. The term "coherence" is used to refer to a person who is in a state of alignment and balance.

In this book we are focused on alignment to the spiritual life force and subtle energy field.

Heart coherence has to do with how you align the physical and spiritual energy of your Heart, with your human transformational journey. This is a very delicate, intricate and at times tricky process.

Throughout mankind's history, different spiritual cultures had their own wisdom traditions which outlined how a person should live, grow and practice spiritually.

They each had their beliefs and practices and most of these groups evolved secluded from other cultures, on different parts of the planet.

For thousands of years these religious groups evolved their own spiritual beliefs concerning what life is about and what the spiritual journey entails. With these beliefs came conflict.

When one group or culture believes their spiritual system to be the only path to truth and another spiritual system believes something different, then both of them are at odds.

This is of course a tragic irony because all spiritual systems seek to create love, peace and harmony. Ultimately, truth has no conflict.

Humankind has created many kinds of divisions which in turn have created conflict and disagreement. Throughout our history, these divisions have ultimately led to war, death and destruction.

The development of many different spiritual systems and beliefs has created deep rifts between various cultures and religions.

In the evolution of Consciousness, which is ultimately the evolution of mankind, we have to move beyond conflict-based beliefs about God, religion and spirituality.

We have to move beyond conflict-based religions that isolate and separate without recognizing the underlying truth of Oneness that is the essence of all paths.

This is where science has an integral role to play in the next stage of mankind's spiritual transformation and evolution.

We now have the ability to measure ourselves energetically, biochemically and neurochemically. We have the seeds that will eventually lead to a more science-based integration of spiritual truth.

This will be a vital part in the quest to resolve the conflict-based spiritual belief paradigm that mankind has been immersed in, since the earliest creation of religious belief systems.

Once you experience unity, you have experienced the essence of reality, which is oneness, love, and happiness. This is real freedom and the foundation of all religions.

What happens is that religions ultimately become discon-nected from this foundational truth and get lost in endless ideas, beliefs and concepts.

Once you experience reality directly without concepts, you know first-hand that separation is an illusion on a quantum energetic level. Therefore quite naturally there is respect and value for all beings no matter what path they practice or how they choose to unfold their spiritual life.

To create religious harmony, there needs to be a common language. There has to be the ability to commune and communicate. The essence of "communication" and the part that has been forgotten is the "communing" part.

Without it people are just talking and bouncing words off one another. There is no aliveness, innate joy or real celebration between people if there is only talking. There is no love in words alone.

Without heartfelt communion between human beings, our interactions are about as fulfilling as dry parched land to a person who is thirsting for water.

There has to be communion – it is the essence of real communication.

In the quest to find a common language through which we can all communicate, science offers a solution. It creates the possibility of unifying what appears on the surface to be many diverse spiritual belief systems.

One example of how science can help bridge this gap between belief systems has to do with a medical health diagnostic method called "heart rate variability". Heart rate variability is the study of how the heart beats. It can be measured by a very simple tool that is connected to a person's ear lobe.

This device measures the blood flow in relation to the heart beat. It is well known in science that heart rate variability is a good indicator of the state of physiological health of an individual.

Variability refers to the capacity of the heart to beat at both the high – end and low-end of a clearly defined scale. In a healthy person, there is a large range.

Let's say you take your pulse and you have an average heart rate of 70. That really does not tell you much of anything. However, heart rate variability tells you the low end of your heartbeat and also the high end.

The difference between the two is how much your heart rate varies from one beat to the next. The greater the variation, the healthier you are.

As people get older, instead of the low end of their heart rate being around 60 and the upper end being around 70-75 there might only be a range of 65-70, which is a very narrow. A healthy person has a heart rate variability of 15 to 20.

Scientific studies have found that shrinkage in the heart rate variability range is an indication of less and less circulation of the blood. This indicates potential health problems that over time may lead to heart attacks and death.

In essence, the smaller the range of your heart beat the greater overall stress your body is experiencing.

Once you are hooked up to this instrument, in just a few minutes, you can see what is happening in terms of your own heart rate variability range.

The reason I am talking about heart rate variability here is that it can be used as an amazing biofeedback device to increase both your overall health and spiritual development, all at the same time.

Getting back to spiritual unfolding in relation to science, we now have an objective tool that gives us a greater awareness of our Heart both physically and spiritually.

Lack of awareness is the essence of all conflict. As awareness develops, so does the recognition of unity along with the awareness that we are all one spirit.

If a group of people get together in a room and start talking about their spiritual journeys, they generally talk about their beliefs, ideas and concepts. They may also talk about their practices, lifestyle and other subjects that pertain to their particular religious system.

Yet, underneath all the surface conversation, what is of real interest is what is happening in each person's Heart rhythm. Heart rhythms that are balanced and coherent form smooth rolling waves when recorded. Heart rhythms that are stressed create very jagged lines.

It would be far more useful in creating effective communication between people, if each individual first brought their heart waves in to balance and harmony before beginning to talk intellectually about any topic.

We should always strive first for Communion then for communication.

If someone's Heart rhythm is chaotic, stressed, and out of sync, then it is impossible for them to share in a space of communion which naturally requires that they be self-aware and present. If awareness is absent, it is also impossible for them to relate to another individual as an expression of One Consciousness.

In short, they would be out of touch with other people in the room and unable to feel unity.

As I was saying earlier the best way to create Unity would be to hook each person up to a heart rate variability device and then to do a short practice to synchronize their heart rhythms.

This would shift the entire energetic- awareness equation in the room. It would take each person away from their mind-based ideas and concepts, which ultimately create division and separation, and give them an aware feeling-based connection. Science can be the bridge to facilitate this energetic connection.

As mankind evolves and transforms as a species, scientific advances and approaches like the one I am discussing will become more and more important.

Science will provide ways to show an individual, what is happening in their heart, neurochemistry, brain and physiology that go beyond simply believing. This will allow people greater insight into how various belief systems and stresses are affecting their life experience.

Such information can be presented to someone in a very objective manner. Thus it would diminish any sense of threat to the individual's ego defense mechanisms.

The communication and sharing would not be perceived as an attack or a personal threat which then allows for greater openness and receptivity to what is being shared.

If you go up to someone and say "you are a really messed up human being" do they simply say "thank you. I agree with that. I will look into it and see what I can do about it"?

Of course not, that is not the response that you would get back for your sharing no matter how good your intention may have been.

When we attempt to share our experience with someone else, it is generally taken in through the filters of the ego. The function of the ego is to protect the individual's sense of self. Therefore, a whole range of defensive responses are likely to occur.

The ego protection mechanisms account for much of the conflict that we experience in relationships of any kind.

When a person is fired up emotionally and energetically they are not able to hear what you have to say. It is not possible for any authentic heart based communication to take place when the walls of the ego are solidly in place. Nor can any authentic change come from such a place of stress and defensiveness.

The challenge is how to deal with all this stress and chaos!

By having an objective scientific way to explore what is happening within a person, you open the door for harmonious, effective sharing and communication to take place. Science simply gives a non-biased presentation of the facts.

If the evidence is science based, you are not in the position of having to believe what someone else thinks about you, your current experience and your behavior. The information comes from an objective source.

By using a diagnostic tool such as heart rate variability you can objectively see how the Heart is beating and functioning in the present moment.

If your heartbeat is relatively fluid and harmonious, the corresponding feeling in the body is one of bliss, happiness and peace, which is reflected in the biochemistry of the body. If you are tense and stressed, your heartbeat will be more erratic and often fast, which creates stress reactions throughout your entire biochemistry.

Thus, it is possible to make an objective analysis of what is occurring within an individual, at any time. Thus the person has a non-biased form of feedback about their current state of being. They can then utilize that feedback to positively shift their emotions and therefore their current experience.

The positive use of science is going to be critical in mankind's ongoing evolution as a species. Eventually we have to find a way to move beyond belief systems that only divide and pit one culture and religion against another.

We need a unified understanding of life and spirit that is based on a nonbiased, open, clear explanation of what actually "is". This is important whether we are dealing with an individual, a group, a corporation or a nation.

This will promote understanding, which leads to greater harmony, compassion and peace.

As we move in this direction, it would also be useful to develop a collective "language" of understanding.

The use of mathematics or numbers does not usually cause heated debates between countries. It is just information. In a similar way we need to move beyond the divisiveness that is caused and generated by our personal spiritual beliefs and our identification with our country, our tribe or our culture.

We need to begin a process of bringing into focus the underlying unity that we all share and carry deep within us.

If we can experience unity within ourselves, it can be shared with others. When many people share their ideas from a place of unity then, quite naturally we will see individuals, societies and countries communicating from a place of equality instead of separateness.

This is just one facet of mankind's evolution at this time. As things evolve and move, forward, it will be interesting to see if we can cultivate a common language of understanding based on science and use it as a key means of communication.

Mankind will never overcome conflict and separation as long as people maintain a perspective and a position based solely upon belief systems.

Heart Coherence...The merging of Science and Mysticism

The essence of this always comes back to the Heart. By bringing a greater focus to an individual's Heart using scientific based technologies, such as heart rate variability, we can assist the person to learn to develop a state of Heart Coherence so that they can create that state whenever it is needed.

An important part of the Awakened Heart Path is the practice of creating heart coherence in each arising moment. This leads to a state of balance. When the Heart becomes coherent, spiritual awareness quite naturally opens and expands.

With practice you can become more self-aware and have a direct experiential understanding of the underlying essence of life. This is much more fulfilling than living unconsciously in a constant state of stress, dis-harmony and separation.

Make it a focus in your life to create a state of Heart Coherency, which automatically creates an atmosphere that is conducive to communion and communication with all those in your world.

CHAPTER SIXTEEN

Living your Life with Spiritual Purpose and Passion

Most people live day to day without any real focus, clarity or direction to their life. They just get up and go about their life as a habitual process.

This way of living life has a flow or continuum to it that maintains a sense of normality; however it does not invite a life that is lived with spiritual purpose and passion.

If you want to awaken to your greater human and spiritual potential, it is important that you live a life that has spiritual purpose and is fueled by spiritual passion.

What is spiritual purpose? Spiritual purpose is recognizing that the purpose of human life is to Awaken. It is to become Consciously Aware that we are Spiritual Beings and all that that entails.

This awareness of who and what we are resides within the depths of each one of our Heart's. It is of the utmost importance then, to live our life day by day with spiritual purpose.

This way of living is in great contrast to a "normal life" where an individual is identified with their life experience and their conditioned sense of self, their persona.

The worldly person, oriented to a normal life, is interested in acquiring things; having wealth, relationships and an assortment of other interests and pursuits.

None of these things in themselves are wrong, but they are devoid of spiritual focus and purpose.

A life that is devoid of spiritual purpose is a life that is basically fruitless. A fruit tree is designed and purposed to flower and bear fruit. Likewise, each human being has within them a deep spiritual dimension that has the innate drive and intention, to flower and bear the fruit of Enlightenment.

This is the fruit of Consciousness and it has many divine aspects and qualities. However, if a person does not consciously embrace Spiritual Purpose, then their life becomes taken up with other concerns, focuses and interests.

Really the reverse should be true. It should be that your life is filled with spiritual purpose which guides you and shows you how to create and structure the rest of your life.

Spiritual purpose informs and instructs you how to align everything you know of as "your life".

Therefore your relationships, your work, your hobbies, how you spend your time, energy and money should all be in alignment with your spiritual purpose. Then you are feeding and fueling this intention that is normally hidden and deeply unconscious.

This deep spiritual intention urges, motivates and pushes you to grow and transform in this lifetime.

Living your Life with Spiritual Purpose and Passion

If you follow, allow and embrace this urge, fulfillment of your spiritual intention and purpose is sure to happen. Just as water cannot help flowing downhill, who you are spiritually cannot help but reveal itself to you if you give it your time, energy and focus.

If you do this, your moment to moment inner Awareness will be filled with divine beauty, peace and happiness. These are the precious gifts of Consciousness that come from living in alignment with spiritual purpose.

People are always looking for miracles, but the greatest miracle is simply being human and having the opportunity to pursue the unfolding of your spiritual nature. This is the Miracle of Awakening.

As you progressively Awaken and evolve, you live your life from a space of Love and Peace rather than from the limitations of human conditioning.

You may think that you have a pretty good life. However, if what you are doing is not in line with your Spiritual Purpose then you will not be able to unfold your full potential. Many traditions consider a human life that is lived without spiritual purpose to be a wasted life.

The spiritual aspect of who you are has such great potential, but you have to choose to live it.

You have to choose to cultivate your spiritual purpose. It doesn't accidentally happen to you and it's not something that is just going to occur by waking up one morning and deciding, "Okay now I'm going to start living my life with spiritual purpose". It is something that has to be consciously chosen on a daily basis.

This life is a gift, an opportunity. However, it will not be of any use to you if you don't actually take the steps and the corresponding actions to bring this opportunity to fruition.

If you make the choice to live your life with spiritual purpose then you need to bring into that intention, spiritual passion.

Passion is the fuel, the desire and the energy that is necessary to unfold the intention of spiritual purpose. Therefore, this passion for transformation has to awaken deep within your being.

It is this awake, aware passion that can direct you to make the changes that are necessary and important in your life. Passion fuels the desire for transformation. Without passion there is just a lackadaisical interest in relation to spiritual purpose.

Thus, spiritual purpose on its own is not enough – you have to have spiritual passion to fuel this purpose and to focus the energy in such a way that you address those things in your life that need to be transformed.

This allows your inner spiritual light to progressively manifest as a living experience.

As you continue to unfold your life with spiritual passion and focused purpose you need to be aware that you will come up against difficult aspects of yourself. You will encounter aspects of your being on an emotional, mental and energetic level that will be felt as resistance and or pain.

At times these deep wounds may cause you to consider abandoning your spiritual purpose. This is normal in the spiritual transformational journey and rather than be discouraged, allow yourself to be encouraged to keep moving inward, onward and upward.

Having spiritual purpose and passion does not mean that your transformation is going to be smooth sailing. It just means that you are committed and clear that no matter what, you will address those aspects of yourself that are in the way of your awakening and that are blocking the experience of your true spiritual Self.

If you go white water rafting down a river or a canyon gorge, you will find that most rapids are rated depending on the degree of intensity - how fast and hard the water flows.

A level one journey is relatively smooth and easy to navigate. A level two journey involves water that is choppy and a little more difficult to navigate. Thus it is more challenging to stay on course.

From there it goes up in varying degrees of intensity to levels where you encounter huge swells and raging white water. With such high levels of intensity your whole being has to be incredibly focused and determined in order to get through the rapids in one piece.

Our human life and journey are very much like that. We have a spiritual purpose which is to flow down the river of life and discover our inner spiritual nature.

We need to have the passion and the will to deal with the varying degrees of intensity that we will most certainly come up against as we travel this river of life. Life at times will be intense. There is no if, ands or buts about it. It will challenge us from time to time and it may become extremely difficult to stay afloat.

It will demand all of our skills, talents and capacity to stay the spiritual course. That is just the way it is.

One reason people go white water rafting, or do other extreme sports, is to come up against something that will challenge them. They are purposely seeking the excitement that forces them to be more focused and present in the moment.

Part of the excitement of human life is that you encounter challenges that require you to develop more of who you are. This may even require you to tap into aspects of your being that you did not know you had.

Each of the challenges we face in life are not there to deter us from our spiritual journey or to make us abandon our desire to awaken fully, but are there to makes us learn about ourselves as well as evolve in the process.

They are there to allow us the opportunity to grow and develop aspects of ourselves that otherwise would lie dormant.

Therefore the challenges that we face in life as we unfold our spiritual purpose, arise to allow us to develop and unfold in a more holistic and balanced way.

Some of these challenges require us to work on the physical body or to deal with our emotional energy and reactions as well as the mind and its self-limiting belief systems. Then there are the trials and tribulations of our personal relationships.

In addition to all of this, we have to deal with our life in general; our environment, our work, and our families – all of these things are important and also very challenging and demanding in their own right.

These are the white water rapid tests, translated into human life.

None of these tests are happening in order defeat us, they are there to make us stronger and more focused so that we continue with our intention for greater growth and transformation.

It is important each day to remind yourself of the fact that you have a purpose to your life. Your purpose is to grow and transform this very day. Your purpose is to become an open vessel that can be filled by Divine Love, Joy and Happiness.

Take whatever challenges you face this day and bring your awareness and focus to them. Then having done that, move forward, move on to the next day and repeat the process.

Apply everything that you know to overcome your life challenges and utilize the passion in your Heart and soul to deal with whatever difficulties you face along this path of human life.

Then as your life continues to unfold over the coming years and decades, you will feel fulfilled knowing that you have lived with spiritual purpose and passion. This in and of itself will bring a sense of joy to your soul.

So many people on the planet do not live their life this way. They are empty and hollow inside. They spend a lot of time and energy doing many different things. However many do so knowing that something is deeply missing from their life.

What is missing is the deep fulfillment that comes from having lived a life directed by spiritual purpose and passion.

There is a profound sense of happiness and peace that comes from knowing you have lived each day of your life with intention and purpose. This is done by giving your best conscious effort to the challenges that confront you moment to moment, while keeping an open, aware, feeling Heart.

Your Heart is your guide as you navigate the white water rapids of life. Listen and attune yourself to your Heart and to your deepest intention. From this place of inner awareness allow your Heart to guide you in the manifestation of your spiritual intention.

It will help you to make better and more consistently positive, life choices. Then as you grow and mature from the experiences of your positive life choices, the inner light of Consciousness will make itself known to you.

This often happens to a person in ways that may appear "magical" but it is simply a result of you having made the choice to live with spiritual purpose and passion.

CHAPTER SEVENTEEN

Meditation, Presence and the Awakened Heart

Each of the aspects above is essential to unfolding ever-greater spiritual evolution and transformation. Meditation in essence, is about being focused and present.

In order for transformation to occur, you have to be focused and present otherwise you are simply at the effect of ego patterns, conditioned from childhood.

These patterns that make up your personality, your "name", are what drive your awareness and therefore your experience. These conditioned egoic patterns do not usually translate into greater spiritual awareness.

If you intend to unfold expansive states of spiritual awareness, love, and wholeness, then it is important to be on a path that includes meditation, because it teaches you to be focused and present.

Most people living a normal life in today's world are not present to the "Presence" of the moment.

They are lost in an endless stream of emotions, thoughts, perceptions and beliefs that lead to the experience they know of as their "personality self".

However, what people know as their personality-self is really the "small self" and very limited in terms of its ability to experience the greater dimensions of Conscious existence.

In order to transform, it is important to embrace and include Meditation, Presence and the Awakened Heart. These are the means to move beyond and through self-imposed limitations to your true spiritual nature.

Meditation is an essential tool and component of this transition.

When you sit for daily meditation, you are attempting to become Present. Plain and simple!

You are attempting to slow down the endless stream of thoughts, feelings and experiences. This is so that you can glimpse a truer reality beyond the filters of your ego.

When you still the mind it allows for an expansion in awareness to occur as well as insight into "What Is" or your essential spiritual nature.

"What Is" isn't limited to the personal self. It includes it and transcends it at the same time.

Even if you are out in the world it is always possible to take a few minutes to meditate, which is simply being Present to what is happening.

If you are at the beach just stop for five to ten minutes and focus on the surf. Just relax into being with the ocean. Notice the shift in your experience when you become present and still.

You can try this practice with animals, flowers and trees also. Trees are very inspirational. It is good to aspire to become like a tree; very grounded, rooted deep in the earth yet able to reach high up into the heavens.

If you can become like a tree you are half way there because being strong and grounded is essential to the journey.

A big problem in today's world is that there is so much activity due to our modern lifestyle and the speed of which everything happens. There is always something trying to grab your attention, which keeps the mind endlessly spinning and distracted

We are constantly engaging in something, processing information, thinking or taking care of some basic task, it is endless.

Unless you make a point to actually stop, sit and be present you are holding a lot of inner stress. This inner stress collapses awareness; it diminishes your ability to perceive and experience a greater reality.

Therefore, it becomes essential to learn how to develop and cultivate Presence. This will assist in the releasing all the various inner stresses and tensions that we normally accumulate in our day to day living.

As you release these self-limiting stresses your Awareness naturally expands into the present moment. We can greatly facilitate this natural process by becoming more centered and grounded in the physical body.

The practices of Tai chi and Qigong are very helpful because they focus on connecting your body with the earth.

When you can connect to the earth energy; it helps to ground the bio-energy of the physical body into the earth, creating a greater connection. This increases your ability to be present and focused.

So much of what you are trying to do on the spiritual journey is to bring yourself down out of the head. Most people's entire life is reduced to living through the mind.

You might have a two and a half thousand square foot home but you are actually living in a one square foot of real estate called your mind.

It doesn't matter what the size of your house is or what you have, what matters is how big your awareness is.

To increase your awareness, you need to focus on connecting into the body and from there connecting to the greater energy field that extends beyond the body.

The first step is to come down out of your head and be present in your body. This is a major step and a transition point for moving into greater awareness and Presence.

A key principle in terms of meditation, presence and The Awakened Heart is to stay in touch with the body. That means staying in touch with what you are feeling and what is happening in your inner world.

Your breath, especially in relation to your solar plexus and the abdominal region, is a direct indicator of whether you are stressed or relaxing into the moment and therefore relaxing into the body.

Take a moment before you read on and check if your abdominal area is relaxed. Put your hand over your abdomen and see if it is naturally moving in and out with the breath.

Is your breath originating from the abdominal region or are you breathing in a shallow way, from the upper chest area?

Being aware of your breath in your abdominal region is really what grounds you into your legs and connects you to the earth.

If your abdomen and legs are tight you are already disconnected to some degree. You are already separated from the balancing energy of the earth.

The analogy that I like to use is that of a tube of toothpaste being squeezed from the bottom. Of course, the toothpaste comes squirting out the top. This is what happens to your internal energy if it is not grounded.

If you are constantly tight in the lower body, you are squeezing and compressing all of your energy up into the head. This in turn creates constant thinking. You become lost in an endless stream of thoughts.

These are real energetics that are taking place in your body and its energy field. This is not some mysterious thing that is happening "to you" it is something you have the ability and the capacity to take charge of and transform.

The first step is to be in touch with your body and breath, here and now. If you are not in touch with it then you cannot begin to take responsibility for it. So first become aware of your body and what is happening within it.

As you continue to transform and unfold, another very important point to understand is that your spiritual journey is not about having any particular experience.

Many people think that the spiritual journey is about having a spiritual experience such as merging into the light, or seeing other worlds and dimensions, feeling ecstatic bliss or developing psychic gifts. These may or may not happen.

The point is, whatever experience you have, even if it is the most glorious spiritual experience, it is still just an experience. Do not become fascinated or obsessed by it.

The real question is how Aware and Present are you right now?

Meditation is not about seeking some experience even if it is the most heavenly experience, it is not about that. It is about your perception in relation to each arising moment.

Your perception determines your experience in the moment.

If you are coming from the perspective that you are a separate human being, separate from Consciousness, separate from love and peace then, you are going to look for an experience to satisfy that lack.

This unspoken belief of "separateness" drives every individual human being's search for an answer to life. It fuels the need for an experience that one day will make you feel whole and complete.

This need and or desire is really not much different than that of sexual desire, which is about seeking the ultimate union experience through sex and orgasm.

With sexual desire, there is an underlying desire to merge, to feel oneness. This desire to merge is what drives human beings to form relationships and to pro-create.

There is an underlying drive and belief that" if I can just have the ultimate sex experience then I can merge through orgasm and I will be fulfilled". Sadly, the search for union outside ourselves, is always a mirage.

Sexual energy is just like a lot of other mundane functions in the body such as the desire to eat when we are hungry. These are just drives and desires that come with being in a human body.

They are neither good nor bad; they are just part of the flow of energy through a human form and they will never lead to the ultimate fulfillment of your Soul.

If you are seeking an experience that you think is going to deliver you from being unhappy, that in itself is an illusion.

Thus a big part of the spiritual journey is about being present so that you can have the discrimination to recognize these subtle programs that are running your life, including your spiritual quest.

It is not to say that having some grand experience of bliss, love and peace is not what you want.

It is just saying that if you experience those states as a separate self ("I" had that experience), then you are already one layer removed from experiencing truthful reality which is absolute Oneness, Conscious Light and Energy.

You are seeing the experience as separate from who you are as Consciousness; it happened to "me", as the ego or personality self.

This can create spiritual vanity and all kinds of problems.

Rather than focusing on experiences, focus on becoming present through the practice of meditation. I am using a broader term of meditation here, not just sitting down quietly in your room. That is just one facet of meditation.

Meditation is being present in every moment of your life. By being meditatively focused, by being present, you can start to become aware of these subtle belief patterns that are driving your search.

As you become aware of these things you can literally feel them and the stress they generate in the body.

You may feel tension in the abdominal region, in the Heart, (the subtle heart not just the physical heart) or become aware of a belief in the mind that is creating a division.

One common example is racial prejudice; having a belief that white people are better than black people or one race is better than another.

Having a belief like that is already creating a division and takes you away from the opportunity to experience Oneness.

It is really important to become aware of the beliefs you hold, and the energy patterns in your body so that you can eventually relax and move beyond them.

Beyond those tensions and belief systems lies that which always is, that which eternally exists.

This is Presence, which is the experience of unity, love and happiness. It is already there, deep within you.

If you are seeking happiness and love either through your work, relationships, hobbies and other things that you like to do then you are missing the point entirely. All these things that make up your life are simply avenues of expression.

However, that expression really needs to come from a state of centered presence and awareness that is anchored deep within your body. Then there is a flowing energy to your expression and there is no "doing" associated with it.

This is where the Heart comes into it. The Awakened Heart is one that is aware of these subtle energies. It is aware of what is taking place within your body's energy field and within the greater energy field.

This field is the universal field of Oneness. Becoming aware of what is taking place within these subtle dimensions, will allow you to become fully present.

That is why the Heart is ultimately the central gateway to Presence.

Certainly, getting your bio chemistry right, looking at things such as your diet, having some type of physical health practice such as yoga, tai chi, exercise, are all important to bring a balance to the body.

Being aware of your concepts and your belief systems is important too. However at the core of all of this, is your

Heart. It is very important to bring a greater awareness to what is happening to the actual energetics of your Heart.

It is very difficult to be present if your body is in a state of constant inner stress and chaos.

If your mind is holding all kinds of divisive, illusionary belief systems and you are emotionally and energetically shut down, it is simply not possible to be fully present and Radiantly Alive.

Therefore, it is important to have spiritual practices that assist in bringing you into a relative state of balance physically, mentally, emotionally.

The trick is, once these dimensions are relatively balanced, you have to let go of them or learn to allow them to be as they are.

Another error on one's spiritual path is to try to perfect any of these dimensions and thereby spending too much time, energy and focus working on them.

You can try to perfect your body, you can try to heal all of your past emotional wounds, you can try to have the purest belief system and keep striving to make these perfect but that's not the point.

The point is to bring them all into relative harmony. This state of harmony allows you to be fully present and aligned.

Once you are deeply connected to Presence, you let go of these dimensions and the energy of consciousness carries you like a raft on a river to the ocean of Oneness.

From that point onwards, the Energy, as felt and experienced through the Awakened Heart, is your direct guide and teacher.

It is a very intricate and subtle process to balance these aspects of yourself to such a degree that it will allow for Presence to fully manifest in and through you.

You can't "do" Presence you can't "make" yourself be present.

But you can practice letting go and taking responsibility for who you are as a physical, emotional and mental human being.

Being balanced allows your awareness to expand and brings the possibility of Self-recognition/ Self-realization. Self-realization is not something that you achieve or someplace you arrive at.

Self-realization occurs and unfolds within your awareness when you have let go of your limited identification. Then the realization arises that you are Consciousness which is inherently happy and free.

When Self-Realization occurs, you recognize that everything you have been seeking, over a lifetime, has actually been a distraction to discovering and unfolding your True Essence.

When that core realization happens there is something in you that fundamentally shifts and let's go.

Once this inner release happens your journey can become relatively easy and natural in its ongoing unfolding, albeit with many inner challenges still to overcome.

Finding this peace and ease allows Presence to become ever more central to your life. This is a critical cornerstone of the spiritual journey.

The purpose of meditation, presence and The Awakened Heart is to become more present to what life really is. It is about uncovering the underlying essence of life and then to live life consciously.

As you become present to your inner Spiritual Essence, your life will progressively find a proper balance and harmony. This in turn creates a sense of peace that you may have been attempting to achieve through other efforts, methods and strategies.

Just like the sunrise, everything in your life gradually starts to brighten. The brightness of your inner reality is revealed. As this inner brightening takes place you realize that a lot of your seeking, doing and effort was not required.

It seems a little bit insane that we have to go through a great portion of our life to realize that we really didn't need many of things that we once firmly believed we did.

We really didn't need the insanity or the stressful effort that engulfed so much of our existence. However, you can't know it until you have reached that point in your journey.

You end up traveling all around the world, move to another country or state, or go from one spiritual community to another until you ultimately recognize that right where you started was perfect.

However, to begin with you couldn't just be there. You had all these energies, conflicts and beliefs inside you that had to be journeyed before this realization and shift in Consciousness could take place.

The trick and difficulty though is that part of you, the ego, does not want that journey to end too soon.

Therefore it will perpetuate the same life ego patterns in an attempt to maintain control of your sense of self, your identity.

This is what happens for as long as you are unaware and unconscious to the tricks and play of the ego. You are held hostage. You are a prisoner to your own suffering and un-enlightenment. That is why we need to become Self-Aware.

It is important to cultivate spiritual awareness through meditation and harmonious Conscious living. This means being focused and present. This is the path to overcoming the ego's wish to remain the same.

Ultimately you must stay sensitized to what is happening in your life, through your Heart. Eventually as you stay focused and present in your Heart you become more aware of what is out of alignment and what needs to be corrected and adjusted in your life.

Much of the time life is demanding that you be somebody other than who you actually are.

For example, you have to be a certain way at your job or you have a relationship based on an un-communicated agreement that, "you be this way" and "I'll be that way" and so forth.

Even with our parents and family, we seldom are our real selves.

We generally walk around wearing many different masks rather than living and revealing our authentic self as it is happening in the present moment.

The simplest way to say this is, if in the moment you are an asshole, then be the very best, most present asshole that you can be. And then be okay with that. It's not about being judgmental or hard on yourself.

If you are feeling stressed or anxious then don't put on a façade that says you are not that way, it simply adds another layer of stress which creates stress on top of stress.

Just say to yourself, I feel in a shitty mood right now and then take it from there. You accept that in yourself because it is how you are actually feeling in the present moment.

You accept that is the condition that you are experiencing right now. And it's okay!

A significant part of the spiritual journey and being able to be present, is the ability to Accept things as they are.

You have to accept the totality of who you are in this Moment. You can't leave out certain facets of yourself.

If you leave out certain facets you end up creating suppression and repression which you feel as stress, limitation and unhappiness.

That stress separates you from experiencing the greater reality of oneness, freedom and happiness. It does not allow you to be Present and open to a deeper reality.

Meditation, Presence and the Awakened Heart

It is important to develop wisdom, discrimination and deeper insight into what it is to be human and how to spiritually transform. These are things that will evolve in you over the course of your spiritual journey.

It all starts with being Present. So just remember this, meditation is about being focused and present in each moment.

Then, as you are Present, you become more aware of your Heart. As your Heart opens and releases its layers of tension, you will become more directly aware of your spiritual nature as Consciousness.

It is all pretty simple, but it takes great awareness and persistence to experience this. Together meditation, Presence and the Awakened Heart will allow a spiritual reality, hitherto unknown to you, to gradually reveal itself.

CHAPTER EIGHTEEN

Being and Becoming...The Paradox of Spiritual Growth and Transformation

This chapter deals with Being and Becoming: the paradox of spiritual transformation and evolution.

Being and Becoming are the two primary aspects of all existence. In India there is a commonly understood phrase, which summarizes the meaning of reality: "Sat Chit Ananda."

"Sat" means being, "Chit" is consciousness and "Ananda" means bliss.

Thus reality is eternal existence, it is conscious and blissful. It is also absolutely free, unbounded and full of unconditional love. Eternal reality is the foundation from which we experience unconditional love, peace and pure awareness.

It unfolds itself in two primary ways: Being and Becoming, which we will discuss now in greater detail.

Manifested reality arises in cycles whereas existence is eternal. It existed before the big bang and will exist after the universe as we know it, dissolves.

Within this current creation of time since the big bang, about 14 billion years have passed. The particles of energy and light and the atoms that make up our current physical body have been in formation for about 14 billion years.

You are very much older than you realize. Someone once said "You are as young as the moment and as old as the universe".

The universe as we know it is probably going to last at least another 30-50 billion years, so really, human life is still just a baby in relation to universal time. Humanity has a long way to go in this current cycle of creation.

The two aspects of eternal reality are firstly "existence" or what we can simply refer to as "Being" and secondly "Becoming" which is the evolution that occurs over time.

These two aspects are the fundamental core of the ongoing transformation of the universe.

The universe started off in a flash then progressively, galaxies, stars, suns and planets were created. This process is ongoing. Consciousness also created human life as part of this play of Reality.

The evolution of the universe is similar to the way a tree grows. Each year, a tree creates another ring around the central core of its trunk. It does this every year of its life and this is how it increases its size.

Likewise, Consciousness keeps building on the previous particle, or the previous atom it has created. It keeps building itself from very simple structures into more complex, intricate structures.

Being and Becoming...

When the frequency of the vibration of light slows down, it forms particles and atoms. Then those atoms coalesce to create cells and the cells create organisms, the organisms create more complex life forms and so forth.

Personally, I find it fascinating that light is the very essence of all manifestation.

Human beings are complex organisms. We are at a very high level of the "becoming" process. Yet it is still a process that continues and it is far from complete.

Therefore, each of our journeys is really about the unfolding of the "becoming" part of the evolutionary process.

The more we become, the more awake we are, the more aware we are, the more we can celebrate the principle of "Sat Chit Ananda" as eternal, conscious, blissful beings.

In order for us to become conscious of this universal process, we have to go through the journey of Awakening.

Most people become stuck in the energetic vibrations and patterns of who they have been in the past. This makes the Becoming part very difficult because their energy becomes rigid and solidified.

Internal spiritual development stops for most people at a fairly early age therefore they are not aware of their spiritual potential. Spiritual transformation by its very nature is extremely subtle and hidden from the ordinary man, woman and child.

The root of this problem is that the Heart becomes de-sensitized in the face of day to day living. The crushing burden of life and the demands of living that most human beings have to deal with are very difficult indeed to successfully overcome.

Thus, most people have forgotten how to grow spiritually with inner Heart-Awareness. Their deeply feeling Heart has lost awareness of the energetics of the present moment therefore very little growth and spiritual development can take place.

In short, people become conditioned and shut down to the deeper levels of their being which effectively strangles the inner "becoming" process.

The Heart has eternal and unimaginable depth to it and it is this depth that you want to cultivate in your life.

This is the "becoming" part. The aim is to create a balance between the "becoming" or evolutionary aspect of your life and the "being" or existence aspect of your life.

There are two fundamental difficulties that human beings face in terms of greater spiritual growth and transformation.

One of these is the tendency, as discussed in previous chapters, to get stuck at ones current level of experience and identity. This is the tendency to simply remain the same. We don't want our comfort to be disturbed in any way and become aggressive in its defense, if it is disturbed.

The flip side of this is trying to create the perfect life, the perfect relationship etc. constantly seeking and striving after the next experience that lies over the next horizon. It can become very exhausting if we are only focused on becoming.

However, the very act of striving after these many and varied things requires time, attention and energy. This always comes at the expense of "Being" and can prevent you from experiencing greater depth and presence in this moment.

All the" Becoming" activity is not very exciting if you do not have a foundation in "Being". Unfortunately, that is what happens to most human beings. We have so many distractions so many demands, that we lose the anchor of Being.

Once you lose the anchor of Being it is difficult to grow in depth. Therefore life is an intricate balancing act between maintaining an awareness of Being in each moment and at the same time allowing yourself to unfold your greater human potential through Becoming.

This balancing act needs to be mastered in order for you to successfully move forward.

A good example of this is someone who performs a hi-wire act, where the high wire is connected between two buildings and there is no safety net.

What is required to complete this act is the ability to be fully present in order to maintain balance while simultaneously keeping the eyes facing forward, towards the goal.

This is very much like the spiritual journey; you have to be very present and aware of where your feet are, in each moment. If you get too busy and distracted, it is easy to make a wrong move and you will topple.

In terms of your spiritual journey, what is sacrificed when you make a wrong move is not just your physical body; it is your spiritual awareness and your transformation.

Many of us live our daily lives as if there are no consequences for our choices. Yet there are very real consequences because how you live each day, determines how your spirit grows and transforms.

If you live your life without being anchored in the present moment you are creating ripples in terms of your "Becoming".

You are diminishing the opportunity to discover and unfold your human potential. However, if you get too focused and fixated on simply "Being" without also being aware of "Becoming" then you will not evolve your spiritual potential.

Life really is an intricate balancing act. Unfortunately, most human beings don't ever consider such subtleties of the spiritual journey.

They just get up in the morning, they go to work, they have their "to do" lists, they get their lists done and before you know it, it is time to go to bed. This is what happens day after day, week after week and month after month.

Most people just keep living within the accepted status quo.

Sadly, the status quo of repetitive action and behavior does not make any space for real transformation. Real transformation always involves the two primary dimensions of Being and Becoming.

It requires that you be fully present and grounded in the body while at the same time look forward and beyond your current level of perception, experience and identity, to the greater evolution of your Soul.

It is of course, your identity, your ego persona which creates your perception and therefore your experience. It is very important to understand this; otherwise you do not recognize how you are actually creating your life in this present moment.

If you want to transform your experience of life, you have to transform your persona and your idea of who you are. When you do that, your perception automatically changes and so does your experience.

For example, in a dimly lit room a person sees a piece of rope and mistakes it for a snake. This sets off a cascade of emotions and thoughts until the person recognizes the error in their perception. Even though what they perceived was not real it affected their experience and thought process none the less.

If you live from the belief that the perception you are having is reality, then there is no space for the experience of pure unconditioned reality to emerge.

I would like to insert an appropriate question at this point for you to consider. What is the difference between conditioned reality and unconditioned reality?

Conditioned reality is constantly putting a flavor, idea and or image onto the experience that is unfolding in the moment.

Your ego, the persona is your conditioned self. It is the product of your upbringing and your experiences from the time of your birth. It is this "self" that puts conditions on each experience that arises. Thus you are conditioning the moment.

Unconditioned reality just is – it has no conditions or filters that limit its expression.

It is only when you begin to move beyond your sense of identity and discover your unconditioned nature that you create the space for change to occur.

When you create that space you feel the freedom and the opening that happens. This is an internal process that is like a light going on in a dark room.

It is important to harmonize your outer life – your relation-ships, your work, where you live and so forth. However, ultimately the greatest work is the process of creating inner space and inner harmony.

The process of unfolding this inner space begins by being present in the moment. That is the "Being" part of the equation. "Being" needs to be the foundation of every moment and brings with it a certain freedom of awareness.

This unrestricted and unconditioned awareness is unchang-ing. It is not defined or limited by your thinking or by what is happening in the moment. A part of you remains anchored in the awareness of Being no matter what is going on in each moment.

Being and Becoming...

Let's say that in the very moment you are reading this sentence, a meteor hits the planet and in a split second everything on the planet is incinerated.

In a single moment the experience you are having of yourself is obviously going to change, however the experience of Being, which is eternal and not limited to your physical form, will not be effected.

Even when this physical body dies the experience of Being, which is eternal, never changes.

It is incredibly important that you awaken to this understanding. This is as simple as noticing that you are alive and breathing.

Become aware of that part of your awareness that does not change. Become aware of that part of yourself that remains unchanged whether you are feeling bad or are having a great moment. This is what is meant by "Being".

As you become aware of this aspect of yourself, it allows you to become anchored in the present moment. When you are anchored in the present moment it is much easier for the "Becoming" part to unfold in a more fluid and graceful fashion.

The greatest amount of energy flows when there is no stress.

Whether we are running an appliance, turning the stove on or listening to music, there has to be a flow of electricity, which is energy, to make it happen. The flow of electricity is the transformational factor that allows us to utilize these things.

Our internal energy, the life force works the same way.

The more present and aware you are the more relaxed and open you become. The more relaxed you are the more the energy channels, meridians and chakras open and dilate.

This creates a greater flow of energy. The more energy that flows through your body, the greater is the potential for spiritual transformation and growth. This is a cascading, domino effect which helps us to unfold our spiritual potential.

However, if you are constantly lost in doing and thinking then you are not aware and present. This will cause you to hold stress and tension on many different levels - physically, emotionally and mentally. You will be unable to just "Be" in Being.

"Being" creates deep relaxation in the Present Moment. This allows the "Becoming" part to unfold much more gracefully and effectively.

When you are constantly busy and unaware, you are pulled from the plug of the universal life force. The irony is that you are the one pulling the plug.

You are doing it by not being present, by not being aware, by not feeling from the greater depths of your Heart which anchors you to Being and Presence in your body.

As you become more present, you dilate and open the energy flow. Then it is the chi, the life force, the prana that evolves you. It is this life force energy that transforms your limited beliefs and releases blocked emotional energy.

Being and Becoming...

To the best of your ability, see if you can balance these two aspects of reality. Being which is about being present and Becoming which is about evolutionary transformation.

Being and Becoming are the Yin and Yang of existence. Both are required for a harmonious and balanced spiritual journey.

Once you master this balance, the magic that is Reality will amaze you. Your life will transform and evolve in the most beautiful and efficient way possible with minimal stress and effort on your part.

CHAPTER NINETEEN

Coming Back to Presence...
A Summary of the Awakened Heart Path

First and foremost, the spiritual journey is about awakening to who you are, to the essential and eternal truth that lays deep within you. This Self-Knowledge is buried in the subtlest recesses of your Heart.

As human beings with a mundane worldly focus we mostly forget this. We forget the underlying purpose to our existence.

Our existence becomes filled with activities, experiences and events that are disordered and unfocused. In general they do not assist us in the unfolding of our greater spiritual awakening.

The Awakened Heart Path is about awakening to the eternal and essential Presence that is directly revealed when we release the egoic stress and contraction surrounding the Heart.

In order to facilitate this awakening, we must each consciously and intentionally embrace our spiritual journey and be willing to overcome any obstacles to this most precious and sacred of endeavors.

The Heart is at the very core of this journey of Awakening. It is the most pivotal and essential component to the successful unfolding of one's spiritual journey.

You can have very profound spiritual and mystical experiences, however unless the Heart and the deeper dimensions of your Soul are consciously awakened and transformed, it is difficult to become integrated and truly whole in these beautiful states of spiritual awareness.

This is what the Awakened Heart is about; it is about awakening to the fundamental Presence that is the very nature of primordial Existence.

The Heart is the gateway. It is the gateway to becoming aware of what is beyond your mind and body.

Paradoxically, you need both your mind and body for this process of Awakening to unfold. Mankind has a tendency to avoid dealing with the challenge of integrating one's mind, body and emotions.

It is extremely important for balanced growth to integrate these different aspects and facets of yourself within the context of ordinary human life.

One error that some people may make in their pursuit of spiritual transformation is to retreat and withdraw from society, relationships, worldly challenges and responsibilities.

The problem with that is you are withdrawing from the mind, body and emotions that must be addressed and transformed in order for the spiritual journey to be fruitful.

By withdrawing into an isolated focus, such as living in a monastery or in a solitary place, you are primarily focusing on the very subtle, internal energy. This often leaves other dimensions of your being untouched and unrefined.

This then creates a limited capacity to unfold in a holistic integrated way. The Heart is the great integrator of all the various aspects that make up your human experience. Without the harmonizing and balancing effect of the Awakened Heart it is very easy to lose ones way.

This issue has been seen countless times in spiritual and religious organizations where a spiritual leader grows in an unbalanced way and their behaviors and actions become distorted, self-oriented and destructive.

Un-balanced growth has the potential to create great harm to the people who are involved with such organizations and spiritual teachers.

One does not have to look far for examples. Catholic priests who have sexually abused children or married evangelical preachers who have affairs with multiple women. The list of course is endless.

Problems arise, when there is a lack of integration of the person's spiritual energy and spiritual awareness, with the balanced Loving Presence of the Heart. This usually results in inappropriate and destructive behavior.

This potential pitfall applies to any individual on their spiritual journey as well as to corporations, governments and even to countries.

The Heart is much more than loving energy, or loving presence, it is what helps to keep your entire being in balance physically, emotionally, and mentally. Without the proper development of the Heart, you can easily create an energetic imbalance.

All imbalances will eventually be corrected either by conscious choice or through the energetic principles of Karma. Over time, unconscious disharmonious patterns, behavior and energy build up like an internal volcano.

Some volcanoes have a slow gentle gradual release that happen overtime, while others have a very intense buildup of pressure and energy.

With the latter, pressure builds and builds and when it finally blows, the energy release can be devastating. Over the course of our history whole societies and cultures have been wiped out by such explosions of energy.

Balanced growth is essential and necessary so choose to anchor your journey of spiritual transformation in the safe harbor of your Heart.

If you develop in a balanced Heart-based way, you are less likely to create an internal buildup of energy followed by an explosion that disintegrates you, your life and the people around you.

The key principle in human transformation is to create balance in all aspects of yourself so that you grow in an integrated way.

Coming Back to Presence...

Remember the Sacred Trinity of Body, Mind and Heart-Spirit. Seek to cultivate these three primary dimensions of yourself so that one dimension of your being does not race ahead of the rest. This will ensure balanced overall growth.

In rare cases an individual may have a spontaneous awakening and have to deal with certain facets of themselves, emotionally, psychologically and energetically, all at once – such things do occur. Most of us however, have a choice as to how we unfold our spiritual journey.

It is important to be conscious of your life choices. Many are not conscious of their life choices so they don't understand why a sudden disruption occurs in their life, creating imbalance and distress for themselves and those around them.

You will always create suffering for yourself when you make unconscious decisions and perform unconscious actions. When this happens learn from it so that you can continue to grow in a positive harmonious way.

This is the principle of Karma at work. It is not that someone is punishing you. It is just the play and manifestation of your choices so that you can learn and evolve.

Caring for the body is the first aspect of the Sacred Trinity. Let's use food as an obvious example of this. An important facet of the transformational journey is to keep the physical body and its bio-chemistry in overall balance.

If you were to eat at McDonald's every day the overall life-force and health of the body would decline. This then affects your energy levels, your ability to focus and your longevity thus limiting your ability to spiritually transform.

The next facet to consider is the emotional dimension. As you grow and transform it is essential to maintain an awareness of what is happening within yourself emotionally.

Most people are aware of the physical body. They are aware that if they do certain things, eat certain things that it affects their experience. Most people are very aware of their thoughts because they are right there, surfacing in their awareness.

However, connecting with the emotional dimension is one of the hardest things for people to do. This is due to years of disconnect from one's deeper energetic feelings and emotions.

The emotional energetic experience has to do with the Heart. The Heart is the bridge between the physical dimension of human experience and the more subtle dimensions that are referred to as mind and ultimately spirit.

Many human beings have created a split between their mind and the physical body because their emotional dimension is repressed, wounded and undeveloped. Therefore holistic integration and harmony is impossible to achieve.

There is an inability for a coherent connection to occur between the physical body and the mind due to the un-addressed emotional dimension. It is like a bridge that is missing over a deep canyon that creates a boundary of separation between two pieces of land.

In most people's daily experience, the body is doing one thing while the mind is off in another universe, doing its own thing.

This leaves little room for feeling deeply into the emotional dimension. Thus the emotions for the most part remain unconscious and are not dealt with except by "crisis" management.

Bringing yourself into holistic emotional balance requires focusing into the Heart, being aware of what you are feeling in each moment of your day, seeing what triggers you, what creates a reaction, what causes you to have an emotional stressful experience and so on.

Transforming with balance requires that you pay attention to all these facets of yourself. It means bringing focus to your physical, emotional and mental dimensions.

This, along with a comprehensive spiritual wisdom system that acts as a compass for your journey, is necessary for balanced growth.

The downfall for most human beings is that they do not have a comprehensive spiritual wisdom system that looks at developing the entire spectrum of human life.

This often ends up leaving parts of a person undeveloped. Balanced, holistic development is required to experience full Enlightenment. Enlightenment is simply the energetic spiritual flowering of the Soul.

The Awakened Heart Path is specifically designed to develop the deep wisdom and understanding that is fundamental to a comprehensive awareness and knowledge of what the spiritual journey involves.

Without a comprehensive spiritual system that integrates and combines all facets of your multidimensional soul, you will end up getting lost and side tracked within the inner experience of the body, mind and emotions.

Sometimes that's just how life is; we have certain lessons to learn, so we have a tendency to get caught up in these sidetracks, or whirlpools of our personal life and our spiritual path.

Like whirlpools in a river, they suck you in and you just end up going round and round in circles, while the rest of the river continues to flow by. At some point when you have circled and processed enough, the whirlpool spits you out so that you can continue your journey.

As human beings we have conscious choice. This is a critical part of the human spiritual experience. As a conscious human being you can intentionally focus and transform these dimensions and facets of yourself so that you can spiritually flower.

You have the choice to work on your limitations and bring them into harmony and balance. This is different from all other animal species on the planet. The animal kingdom simply lives by stimulus and response. They cannot plan things years in advance like we do.

They do not think "this is a dry season so I need to grow a certain type of plant that will allow me to have food for the next several years." They just live in the present moment and follow habitual patterns and instincts to survive.

The capacity we have to contemplate and consider past experience is what gives us a huge advantage in life - if we make use of it.

However, most people live in a state of automaticity just like the rest of the animal kingdom. A lot of time human beings do not use their intelligence fully.

They do not demonstrate a high degree of evolutionary awareness even though they have great potential. This to me is a huge waste of the gift of human intelligence.

Intelligence is the ability to contemplate and consider your evolutionary transformation.

Intelligence isn't sitting down and being able to work out the mathematics it takes to go to the moon, or to build a computer. That's a limited definition of intelligence, it's a mental intelligence and yes it is useful.

However, what you want to cultivate in your life is evolutionary intelligence.

It allows for you to consider and reflect in each moment and to ask yourself "How is this affecting my spiritual transformation, how is this affecting my human experience? Am I progressively cultivating a better life, a holistic life?" and so on.

This brings into the picture an understanding of *holism*, synergy and integration. To create a holistic life, you have to look across the entire spectrum of your physical, emotional, mental, psychological, and energetic field of experience. Then apply evolutionary intelligence to your choices.

When you use your intelligence in a proper way, you can effectively unfold your spiritual journey, rather than leave it to circumstance, chance and hope.

There is always the possibility that anyone, anytime, anywhere can awaken and be free from the illusionary identification of the ego persona. However, most people live their entire life trapped in that limited identification.

They live in identification with the ego. The ego is nothing but the composite of past conditioned experience that colors one's moment to moment awareness and experience.

When you are born you are given a name. At first your name has no baggage with it. However, by the time you are an adult, your name includes all the experiences that you have grown up with.

It represents who you know yourself to be based on your life experiences and conditioning. The egoic persona is the movie that the light of consciousness, or self-awareness, is projected through.

Your ego persona is really just the film. When you go to a movie and look at the movie screen, you only see the film projected onto it. You are not seeing anything different on the screen than what is contained in the film itself. That is what ego identification is.

All your conditioned experiences become your personal ego movie, complete with sound, visuals, body sensations and energetic feelings. This is your ego film, and the light of consciousness is projected through it.

It becomes the way you experience the world. What you are watching through your eyes, through your awareness is nothing more than the conditioned past, playing out on the "screen" of the present moment which is pure awareness.

Enlightenment then, is recognizing that you are the Light, the Consciousness and not the ego film. This truly is Awakening to Reality.

People generally make their choices based on the conditioned past. To a certain extent this is necessary. It is part of learning and growing and brings you to a point where you can reflect on and contemplate your choices.

If you are not reflecting and contemplating beyond the ego film that is creating your experience in the moment, then you will continue to make limiting choices throughout your entire life span.

There is no opportunity for a profound awakening, for a profound shift in your internal awareness if you are identified with your persona and its film. When this is the case, your external awareness is always a reflection of the internal egoic processes moment by moment.

It can't be any different than this until an individual Awakens to their innate inner freedom prior to mind and conditioning.

When they do, life becomes a process of conscious cultivation and development rather than something that is akin to winning the spiritual lottery.

Otherwise, like wanting to win the lottery, you just hope things will happen. You just hope you will become happy; you just hope that somehow your life is going to work out. That is how most people live their life.

If you look at humanity en mass can you say that strategy works very well? It is easy to see that generally it works very poorly.

2012 and beyond has to do with a greater collective awakening.

If you want to make sure that you are a participant in the collective awakening, you have to apply wisdom, you have to consider and contemplate your life and make choices that will align you to the coming energetic changes.

For the most part, this is not how humanity chooses to live. Generally people consider their life from the perspective of how they can make more money, how they can plan for retirement, how they can meet someone and have a great relationship and so on.

Very few people orient their life around the primary intention of Consciousness which is to Wake up and Evolve.

If you forget this then the majority of your time, energy, resources, money, the choices you make, the associations you have etc. will not support your Awakening. That is just the way it is.

However, since you are reading this you have a choice to make a difference as to how your life unfolds. What will you do with this information? Will you ignore it, deny it and hide it away in the closet? There are many options.

If you do decide you want to unfold your life through conscious choice with evolutionary intelligence, then that is going to require what has been called the "the hero's journey".

The hero's journey is about having the courage, the focus, and the determination to keep moving, to keep growing, to keep unfolding.

The truth is that it is a very difficult, even horrifying, painful and terrifying process to wake up at certain stages of the journey. That's the truth and that's the way it is.

Other times, when you unravel and heal a part of you that has been dysfunctional, hidden and or traumatized you may become exhilarated, ecstatic, blissful and peaceful. Then you will know from direct experience that yes you can grow, transform and evolve.

This happens whenever you release something that has been a limitation to unfolding the greater awakening of your soul.

That really is what the hero's journey is about. It is what is required on the Awakened Heart Path. It is about having the courage to look at those aspects of yourself that may not be pleasant and finding a way to overcome any challenges.

The Awakened Heart Path also addresses the practical side of your development, such as diet, dietary supplements, your environment, the air you breathe and the water you drink and so on.

It explores and examines your emotional experience, your mind and psyche. It will also assist in the cultivation of subtle spiritual energy through various practices and methods.

This book outlines the foundational principles and keys for holistic, balanced, spiritual growth and transformation through Heart-Centered Awareness and Presence.

If you follow these principles your inner journey will be much smoother and far more fruitful.

It will assist you to grow in love, to progressively become love and to then share the love that you have always been. This is the intention of this book.

I am delighted to have shared these principles of spiritual transformation with you in this present moment. If you feel a resonance with what has been shared here and would like further assistance and guidance, then please go to the website www.awakened-heart-path.com

May your spiritual path be illuminated by the Awakened Heart.

APPENDIX ONE

Foreword to the
Awakened Heart Mastery Course and Services

This book, The Awakened Heart Path, is an introduction to the ideas, principles and methods developed by Kevin, over 25 years of personal spiritual exploration.

It is a great start but is only a first step.

Therefore, Kevin has created a 16 week online video course that will guide and instruct you on how to more effectively unfold The Awakened Heart Path for yourself.

Following, in appendix 2 and 3 are transcripts from the Intro to the Awakened Heart Mastery Course and Week 1 of the Awakened Heart Mastery Course for you to read as well These videos can also be watched at www.Awakened-Heart-Path.com.

The remaining pages outline other services that Kevin offers. These may be of assistance to you if you desire personal guidance, direction and spiritual empowerment.

APPENDIX TWO

Intro to Awakened Heart Mastery Course

(Transcribed from the video introduction that can be found online at www.awakened-heart-path.com)

This course is designed to be of practical assistance in implementing the spiritual wisdom outlined in the book "The Awakened Heart Path".

What is the Awakened Heart Mastery Course?

The Awakened Heart Mastery Course is about unfolding your Spiritual Essence. It is about unfolding who you are as a spiritual being so that you can live and experience what that is.

The course is experience based so that you discover for yourself what it is to be a spiritually aware and awakened human being, rather than this being just a concept that you hold in your mind.

It is important to make the transition from merely thinking and knowing that you are Spirit or Consciousness, to actually implementing that experience in your daily life.

Once this transition occurs, you will begin to experience yourself as Consciousness in a more tangible way.

In short, this course is designed to assist you to unfold your intention for greater spiritual awakening and self-realization and to give you the tools to be able to live that day by day.

In this way, experiencing the love that you are is no longer a theory - you can grow, share and participate in it. That is what the Awakened Heart is really about. It is about discovering the love that transcends time and space.

Certainly one avenue of experiencing love is relational love - the love that you have for your spouse or your significant other or for your children or parents.

Relational love is just one form of love. The Awakened Heart is really about awakening to spiritual love. This love is eternal and is what will remain after everything else disappears.

Even though your body will pass away someday, the spiritual love that emanates from an Awakened Heart will always exist.

Thus whatever progress you make in this current lifetime is something that will be with your soul for all time. That is why I encourage all souls, who have an interest in their further development and awakening, to actually do something about it.

Get beyond just reading about it. Move beyond just reading the spiritual texts be it the Vedas, the Bible, the Koran or other spiritual material that you have seen out there. Get down to actually living your transformation.

Live your life in such a way that you are evolving your capacity to be present as a spiritual being so that who you are as Consciousness, can find an avenue of expression through this human form.

In order to facilitate such change, you have to be a conscious participant of this journey. You have to be willing to transform who you are in your totality, to become a living conduit for the Divine. When you do this, the Divine can fully express, live and love through you.

For this to occur there has to be an inner structure. The Awakened Heart Mastery Course gives you the tools, methods, wisdom, insight and understanding that facilitate your intention to become an expression of the Divine.

This is real mastery. Real Mastery is about the spiritual flowering of your soul. People can be masterful in many areas of life however the most important area in which to be masterful is your spiritual unfolding.

I like to consider the totality of our being as a beautiful symphony. A symphony is played by an orchestra composed of many different instruments. For the performance to be harmonic and flowing, all the instruments have to play the same bar of music with precision and timing.

We are each an expression of different facets of consciousness which can be likened to the instruments of an orchestra. These are known as Body, Mind and Heart-Spirit. They are the three primary dimensions that I refer to as the Sacred Trinity.

The body is this physical body, its biochemistry and its overall health. The mind is your mind and the all concepts and beliefs that are held there. The last and most important dimension is your Heart and the spiritual energy that emanates from it, when it is open.

The Heart is the living pump that with each heartbeat transmits the energy of spiritual consciousness.

From there that energy travels via the blood and other energy channels throughout the whole body. It is what lives the body. A person is alive as long as their heart is beating and human life begins only a few days after conception, when the heart begins to beat.

As this course progresses we will look at how to fine tune these instruments; the Body, the Mind and Heart-Spirit. They are important as they make up your life experience.

This Mastery Course will explore in detail, the inner dimensions of your psyche. We will look into those dimensions of yourself that have been conditioned and programmed since birth with beliefs, ideas and emotional energies that are creating interference patterns to your greater spiritual awakening.

To create overall harmony, all of these parts of your being need to be examined and made conscious. There will be practices to assist you to do this. Many of the practices shared during the course, will help you to be more focused, present and aware.

These are the foundational skills that are needed if you are going to be successful in your quest for greater spiritual transformation.

First and foremost you have to learn to be focused.

Due to the hectic, crazy pace on the planet today, most people's focus is very fragmented. If you have a fragmented focus you do not have the power and the ability to penetrate into the greater depths of your being.

When the rays of the sun are focused through a magnifying glass they can ignite a piece of paper or a leaf. Likewise as you sharpen your focus you can burn away the dysfunctional patterns that are creating the experience of suffering and limitation in your life.

As most of you know, our planet as a whole is not a very conscious, aware, place to live. The mass population that makes up the planet is for the most part deeply asleep to their spiritual potential.

In order to activate the deeper spiritual potential that exists within you as a human being, you have to have the ability to focus.

This is the first step. Once you train your focus and make it stronger it can penetrate through the layers of physical, emotional and mental patterns that act as an interference to the inner radiance and light of Consciousness.

This is in essence what you are doing when you unfold spiritually. You are creating a transparent vessel so that the light of consciousness can shine through it.

In order to do that the three dimensions of Body, Mind and Heart-Spirit, have to be purified, harmonized and clarified.

Once you have developed your focus, the next stage to concentrate on is expanding your awareness. For the most part people are not even aware of what is going on energetically in their physical bodies let alone being deeply aware of the subtle energy of their spiritual body.

To assist with this we want to expand and develop your awareness and move it out of the head, down into the body and center it in the Heart. Therefore as you move through this course some of the practices will directly target your ability to be present and centered in the Heart.

As you become more present in the Heart you will also become more aware of your feelings from a heart level. This is not just in reference to your emotional feelings but also to your spiritual feelings and your deeper spiritual energy.

When you come out of the head and into the heart you will be more directly aware of where the obstructions and blockages are in your being. This is a gift because you cannot transform that which you are not aware of.

As you move more deeply into the course you will be developing the capacity to become present as Heart feeling awareness. This is the core to unfolding your inner spiritual mastery.

As you start to develop your capacity to be present and feeling from the center of your Heart and to be present in your entire body, you will be able to take greater responsibility for those patterns within yourself that are disharmonious. It is a natural and logical progression.

Once that occurs you can begin working on the more subtle obstructions, contractions and blockages which have to do with your psyche and the subtle psychic energy field of your mind, concepts and beliefs.

Many times people try to work on their beliefs and concepts without first being anchored and present in their body and in their Heart.

However, doing the work in that order is often not effective. This is because many of the beliefs and concepts that are self-limiting are tied to an energetic contraction in the body.

If you are unaware of the deeper feelings in your Heart and the deeper energy flows that exist within the body, then you are not able to connect to the energetic "charge" that is creating the obstruction in your consciousness.

This is why it is important to first become grounded, aware and present in the body and the Heart. Once this occurs you can begin to become aware of the subtle psychic imprints and the subtle psychic belief systems you are holding onto, all of which create an obstruction to the light of consciousness.

This is a critical and much subtler form of transformation as it deals with being able to sense energy in relation to thoughts and beliefs. Each thought is one that allows light through, blocks it or is a mixture of the two.

As you take responsibility for your human body, your mind and the emotional energies that you experience, you will be able to consciously choose thought patterns and feelings that allow light and Consciousness to come through.

This is the beginning of human mastery. It begins with being aware and leads progressively to being responsible for all that you are as a human being.

This course is really a beginning step on an ongoing path and the first of more courses to come.

This first 16 week course will provide you with the foundational stepping stones that will help you make use of future courses.

We have to start with the very basics which are your focus, your awareness and your ability to be present because it is from there that all the rest of the transformation takes place.

If this course interests you I welcome you with an open Heart, with open arms and look forward to your greater awakening and personal mastery.

Kevin Hunter.

APPENDIX THREE

Awakened Heart Mastery Course Week One

It is with heartfelt joy that I welcome each one of you as we continue the exploration and the unfolding of your Spiritual Heart.

This is the first practice session week of the Awakened Heart Mastery Course. Welcome! May your heart continue to open and flower.

The Awakened Heart Mastery Course is designed to facilitate your greater awakening. In some spiritual traditions they refer to this as enlightenment or self-realization.

Enlightenment in the traditional understanding is recognizing who you truly are as conscious presence and unconditional love.

Who most people think they are and what they experience themselves to be, is not who they truly are.

This statement may seem very confusing. However, from the time we are born we start to develop a sense of identity which becomes the foundation from which we journey our life until this body passes away.

This identity otherwise known as the ego seems real but it is not our true self. For the most part, people do not awaken to their spiritual self within a single lifetime because they are so heavily identified with their ego, their personality–self.

Spiritual paths were developed to assist people to awaken to the deepest part of themselves, which is divine and eternal. If left to our own devices, we tend to focus only on what is temporary and transitional and do not move beyond the personality-self.

In the past, many spiritual traditions focused purely on the transcendence aspect of spiritual mastery. Therefore the practices were designed to help a person discover who they are as Consciousness, but there was little emphasis on integrating those experiences into the person's daily life.

For hundreds of years on this planet the lifetime expectancy for a human being was between thirty to forty years old. Most people did not live into their seventies, eighties and nineties. These days to live to be one hundred years old is no longer a rarity.

In the past due to the short lifespan, the emphasis had to be solely on awakening to who you are as Consciousness. There was little time to get beyond that stage of the journey.

As many traditions have described, Consciousness is self-existing. In other words, it is not dependent upon having a physical body to exist. It exists independent of this body and this lifetime and is in fact what creates all manifestation, including this physical body.

The ancient wisdom traditions understood the inherent qualities of Consciousness to be as follows:

First and foremost, Consciousness is unlimited freedom. It has no limitations.

Normally we experience life in this body as having many limitations. A common example of this is waking up one morning and finding that your body is aching all over and you have a fever.

Additionally as the body gets older it no longer functions as well and you begin to notice its limitations and restrictions.

The same applies to our minds. Most people experience various limitations in the way their mind thinks. The mind thinks in repetitive cycles. It is like playing the same record over and over again and at times it can be enough to drive a person crazy.

I am sure many people would like to take their mind and throw it in the trash can at times. If only it was that easy. If only the mind were a CD and we could just take it out of the CD player and set it aside. Unfortunately, the human spiritual journey is not constructed that way – it is more complicated.

Additionally, most people feel at the mercy of their emotional experience. Something happens that triggers a reaction and they feel angry, upset, afraid, or sorrowful. There is a wide range of potential emotional experience.

The thing to notice is that the normal experience people have physically, emotionally and mentally, is generally characterized by a sense of limitation.

It is a feeling of being confined, limited and restricted to a physical body that exists within time and space. Therefore all traditions looked at how to free a person from this sense of limitation.

If the fundamental quality of Consciousness is freedom with absolutely no limitations and if that freedom comes along with the experience of eternal existence , unconditional happiness and unconditional infinite love – then we have to ask why there is such a discrepancy between that and our normal everyday experience.

In other words, if this is a true description of reality why then are we having such a limited experience? In essence the experience of limitation arises because of our egoic identity.

This identification has been imprinted from birth. If you choose to look at it from a larger perspective, the identification is the result of imprints from many lifetimes. It is all based on conditioning.

Therefore everything that is arising in your awareness is based on a conditioned limitation. That limitation, which comprises our body, our mind, our thinking and our feelings, in and of itself is not reality – yet we take it to be reality.

How many people actually question what reality is?

Most people just accept that what they are experiencing is reality. If you want to change the experience you are having then you have to look at how it is created. You have to look at why the same experience keeps happening.

Every time you go to sleep you wake up. In the morning when you wake it is "you" that's there it is not somebody else is it? It is not somebody else's life. You wake up and there you are again and you live that day within the sense of constriction caused by your conditioning.

These patterns, this experience that you are having, this perception of reality that you are having, can be shifted. That is the first point that you have to recognize otherwise you condemn yourself to a life of limitation.

When you accept as truth; that the experience you are currently having is not the experience of reality, then it can be transformed.

Thus the spiritual journey is about transformation. What we are transforming is what we have known as our ego. It is extremely important to understand that the ego is not just your mental sense of self

The ego is fundamentally a sense experience. It is a sensation that you are having. That sensation is that your body feels separate from other things.

It feels separate from other people, it feels separate from the chair you are sitting on, it feels separate from the car that you drive and it feels separate from people that you are in relationship with.

Therefore, the fundamental underlying experience of the ego is separation.

So first and foremost you want to cultivate an awareness of this sense of separation because everything else is an add-on to it.

All your thinking about yourself and about your life, all the emotional experiences that you are having, everything that you are feeling physically, is all rooted in this core feeling of separation.

From the moment that you wake up in the morning, you experience yourself as separate. That is the foundation of the experience that you are having every moment

The truth of reality is that there is no separation. This is even described in quantum physics. The experience of separation is a "conditioned experience" – it is not the experience of reality itself.

This conditioning can be transformed and as you walk the spiritual path you will notice a gradual diminishing of it.

The sense of separation is progressively replaced by a sense of unity and love that does not come from outside yourself. It is not arising because someone loves you; it is arising because it is the nature of your true inner self.

When you wake up in the morning, you are aware. It is not because something is making you aware; awareness is simply the foundational quality that arises when you wake up. Awareness is inherent – it is a fundamental quality of Consciousness.

Likewise love is another foundational quality that lies within you. It does not have to have a reason to be there. It is there, always. It is just that we obstruct the experience of what is already deep within us.

This obstruction is what the ego continuously creates, if you do not transform it. The ego or personality self is simply an obstruction to Reality.

Therefore if we are going to experience reality as it actually is, we have to take on the journey of transforming our limited sense of identity, our ego.

Once again notice that I am not just emphasizing the ego as being a mental sense of self. It is first and foremost the actual experience that you are a separate being.

This always has to be your foundational understanding of spiritual transformation:

The experience of separation, of yourself as a separate being, is the core of your ego. Everything else around that, your mind, your emotions, the various feelings that you are having, is simply the "play" of that sense of separation.

This is where your focus has to be. Your understanding of the ego as the sense of separateness has to form the foundation of your spiritual path. If this is not the foundation, then all the practices that you are doing, even if they are "spiritual" or "religious" are being done as a separate ego.

Because of that, they will never awaken you. The reason being, that they are not dealing with the fundamental root problem of your experience of separation. You are just practicing as the separate ego, which can create all kinds of spiritual egotism.

So at the very core of your spiritual journey you have to maintain awareness of this sense of separation, moment by moment. Also be aware of how your mind comes in to validate this perception and how it justifies and reinforces it.

The Awakened Heart Mastery Course is really about assisting you to shift these patterns and to start to transform them. As we go through this course we will be taking things step by step.

However, in any moment you can be directly aware of reality, in any moment you can be directly free. Any moment that you are feeling deep into your Heart and you are aware and present is a moment of freedom. That is a moment of unconditioned reality.

Therefore, this is always the most important focus and practice. Regardless of whatever else the course will address, this understanding that has been shared with you right now is in essence, The Awakened Heart Mastery Course.

We inhabit a physical body, with a conditioned mind and we experience a multitude of emotions on a daily basis that seem to belong only to ourselves.

All of these aspects need to be harmonized and brought into alignment so that the truth of what lies beyond the experience of separateness can eventually shine through.

If I were to say to you now "Go beyond your experience of separateness", you can't do it, there is too much in the way. There is too much conditioning.

If you can go directly beyond the experience of separateness right now, then you don't need the rest of this course. You can ask for a refund and we will celebrate our oneness together. However, if you are unable to do that, then I suggest that you continue with it.

The very first step beyond what I shared with you as the essential wisdom of moving beyond separateness is to understand that we are comprised of three primary dimensions which I refer to as the Sacred Trinity.

This is not the Sacred Trinity of religious teachings of the Father, Son and Holy Ghost; this is the Sacred Trinity of what I call Body, Mind and Heart-Spirit.

This is the real Sacred Trinity because it is through these three primary aspects of our human existence, that we experience life, interact with life, move through life and hopefully grow and transform.

So what is creating our sense of separateness?

It is how our physical body, our mind and our emotional experience, as well as the spiritual energy which I call Heart – Spirit are interacting with one another in each moment.

What normally happens to people is that this Sacred Trinity becomes out of alignment and this makes it very difficult for a person to be present.

If you cannot be present, you can never be aware of the underlying sense of separateness which has its origin in the Heart.

The Heart itself is the core of what is generating the sense of separateness because it becomes obstructed and constricted. For most people the awareness of this primal Heart contraction is absolutely unconscious.

Scientists say we use two or three percent of our brain; we are also using about that much of the potential that our spiritual Heart is capable of.

Our Heart is like a camera lens: it can either be open, shut or somewhere in-between.

A very important part of the spiritual journey is to open the camera lens of the Heart wide because then the energy of Consciousness, the vital life force, can flow through it unobstructed.

Once this flow happens, the sense of separateness gradually diminishes and eventually disappears altogether.

So we are looking at how we can open and increase the flow of energy through the Heart center. When I refer to this area I am not just talking about the physical heart or the heart chakra. The chakras and the meridian systems exist on different levels of energy.

What I am talking about when I refer to the Heart center is the seat of the soul – it is the doorway between pure, unconscious manifestation and everything that is about to become manifest – it is the doorway of "being" and the "becoming" that is at the center of the Heart.

The essence of our spiritual transformation comes down to moving beyond the deep unconscious energetic contraction in the Heart. There are however multiple challenges to this undertaking.

One challenge is that this contraction and sense of separateness is constantly being reinforced by the physical body and one's thinking processes that convince us that we are indeed separate.

Since most people cannot be directly aware of the core contraction in the Heart there needs to be a progressive path that allows one to become more aware and present to the sense of separateness itself.

The first step and what we are focusing on this week is becoming more present. This really is the foundation to transformation.

You cannot transform your life if you are not present to it.

Secondly, you cannot be present to things that you are not yet aware of.

Lastly, you cannot be aware and present if you are not fully conscious of the physical body.

This path of the Heart, the Awakened Heart Path is about embodied awareness of your spiritual essence via the doorway of the Heart.

Thus the initial step to becoming present is being aware of the physical body. You have to ground your awareness in something because for the most part – where is your awareness? Which is really asking where is your focus?

If you are like most people, your focus is lost in an endless stream of mental concepts; it is lost in an endless stream of thinking that does not allow you to be present.

If you cannot be present you cannot be aware. If you cannot be aware you cannot locate that sense of separation and feel beyond it to your true essence.

Therefore the first essential step is becoming present in the body, becoming grounded and connected to the physical body.

Unlike some spiritual systems that look to take awareness up and out the top of the head and leave the body behind, we are taking a different approach; we are working at becoming fully present in the body.

We are using the body as a tool; we are using it as an anchor for our awareness.

Rather than look at the physical body as something to go beyond and to get rid of, we are looking at it as a valuable gift.

In the Sacred Trinity our physical body is a great gift and it is the first step on the Awakened Heart Path and to Awakened Heart Mastery.

Mastery is about being focused and fully here in this present moment.

In the Sacred Trinity, the body is most represented by the energy center that in the Zen tradition is called the Hara or in the Taoist tradition called the Dantien.

If you are familiar with the yoga tradition, this relates to the first, second and third chakras – which we are taking as one energy center.

This energy center, the hara, reflects the vital life force of the physical body. So first and foremost we want to work with this – we want to bring more life force into the body.

The more life force energy we bring into the body the easier it is to be grounded and the easier it is to be present.

Otherwise what happens is that the abdominal hara region remains tight and constricted. This energy contraction causes the life force energy to be pushed up to the head.

Have you ever seen one of those kid's toys that has a wheel and the wind blows it and makes the wheel spin? Well that is basically what happens when the energy in the hara is blocked.

Energy will always go somewhere, so if it is blocked from going somewhere in a balanced way it will go somewhere else. In this case, that "somewhere else" happens to be the brain / mind.

Generally, due to the energy blockages in the hara region, people's internal life energy is pushed up into the brain which makes the neurons and the brain cells work in a stressed, imbalanced way.

When this happens, what do you notice in your awareness, your inner experience?

The result is that there is a constant stream of thoughts and there is no peace or presence.

Therefore the first part in unraveling the energy system is working with the hara – it is about bringing your focus down and anchoring it in the hara.

This area includes the kidney region, the genitals and all the way up to the solar plexus – so it is this whole region that we are focusing on.

Our practice today is a 5 minute exercise. What I would like you to do is to focus your awareness, your attention down into the navel area, but also be aware of the entire abdominal region, the kidneys, the lower back - just let all your awareness be right there.

You can either close your eyes or keep your eyes halfway open. You do not really want to look at anything outside, but at the same time for some people if they close their eyes they have a tendency to go up into the brain and third eye – so just see what feels more comfortable for you.

Then I want you to focus solely in that area. At this point of the practice, I am not going to add in any techniques that would help to clear this area because the first step is always awareness.

As we go through this mastery course we will be referring to an acronym or method that I call A.C.T .

A.C.T. stands for Awareness, Cultivation and Transformation. You have to "A.C.T." if you want to transform your life.

The first step in any practice is always awareness – before you start anything whether it is a yoga or meditation session, or any other technique or method, bring awareness to it.

This is what we are really doing today- we are just bringing and awareness to an energetic center that most strongly correlates with the physical body's vital life force.

Go ahead and put your focus there now and keep it there for the next five minutes. If you notice that your awareness drifts away from that area then just bring it back again. After 5 minutes we will review your experience.

So now that the session has ended, take a moment to reflect on your experience.

What I would like to do is to go around the room and have you share what you noticed. If you did not notice anything that is fine, just share whatever your experience was. In this way we can help refine this first practice which is about grounding into the hara.

So we will start over here:

Participant 1: I didn't notice too much I just noticed how I am in this area. I lost concentration and was unable to stay there.

Kevin: That is probably going to be the first thing that many people will have difficulty with - maintaining their concentration. We are so conditioned to being aware of our thinking, which has no anchor. It is just like the wind. You cannot really anchor your focus in the wind. This challenge of maintaining concentration on a certain area is going to be a normal challenge for most people.

Participant 2: My experience was emotion – almost like a connection to life, to a strong force and my mind sort of dropped away and I just concentrated.

Kevin: OK great. That is a very good example of what happens as your focus moves out of the mind. That is exactly what will occur for some people. You will have this sense of the mind becoming more still and more spacious. This can even progress into a very strong life force feeling and vibration.

Over time as you develop the ability to focus you will notice a greater quieting and stilling of the mind. Since the mind isn't being given the same amount of energy as usual it won't spin in the same way and it won't distract you in the same way.

Participant 3: I noticed that when I focused in the Hara that there was a flow of energy in a counterclockwise direction. If I was to let my focus waiver I could feel the energy want to move up and then I would have to bring myself back down to the hara area. Then I noticed that I could direct myself into different areas of the hara and just be comfortable feeling what was occurring inside as I moved my focus around.

Kevin: Good, if you connect with the energy you can get that sense of energy movement clockwise or counterclockwise because of the different meridian channels there and due to the chakra system.

It really is the life force and vital energy system for the body. Sometimes the energy can grow to be quite strong there and at other times you may just notice a sense of stillness but again it is the first step so… alright.

Participant 4: I noticed just towards the end a kind of blurring the lines of body and chair and I don't want to say Oneness because that's not it, but just that the sensation wasn't there. It was sort of a blurring a numbness and not really aware that I was sitting in my chair and not being worried about what my body was doing.

Kevin: Were you able to keep your focus there or did your focus also wander?

Participant 5: Well it wandered. Towards the end it was a little easier but it was like monkeys on rings.

Kevin: Remember that the key to this course is going to be the application of the practices. This is best symbolized by the acronym ACT – Awareness, Cultivation, Transformation.

It's going to take practice. For the entire week one of the course I recommend that you take at least 10 minutes a day and do this practice of focusing into the hara.

Take at least one or two weeks to develop this. As we go along the course we will be integrating these practices into a more unified practice. To start with you need to practice keeping your focus present in the hara. Okay good.

Participant 6: I used my breath to keep myself present and when my mind wandered I would just use the breath again. As I used the breath to stay down in the hara, I noticed a heartbeat down there. It's not that I got still but I was able to stay down there with the breath. So I used the breath and it was powerful.

Kevin: It's interesting what you were saying about the second heart beat. In the Taoist tradition they actually refer to the abdominal region as the second heart. As we get further along in the course we will be using certain breathing techniques that synchronize the hara with the heart.

When you use the abdominal region in a coherent manner it helps to relax the Heart and to synchronize the energy channels from the heart down to the abdomen. There is a core energy channel that connects from the abdominal region up to the Heart.

As we progress further in this course we will be working with these deeper energy centers. The system that I like to work with is known as the eight extraordinary channels. It comes from a Taoist system of practice.

I find it really connects the practice of the Sacred Trinity very effectively. We will be working with these methods as we go along.

Participant 7: At first I could feel the energy in the hara and then the mind would come up....and it sort of went back and forth. When I let the attention rest a lot of time I would have little pops in there and could feel the energy there.

Kevin: OK good I think we have talked about that. It is going to be normal as you learn to develop focus to find your attention going back and forth. The other thing to point out about grounding the energy in the Hara is that it is the most effective and direct way to still and quiet the mind.

Eventually we will be doing standing exercises which will help you connect the hara to your leg energy channels and from there to connect to the earth.

Another adjunct to this practice of focusing in the hara, which I highly encourage, is to do this practice for 10 minutes outside with your bare feet on the earth.

A lot of times we are disconnected from the earth energy because we wear shoes and we are indoors a great amount of time. When we are indoors we are exposed to very chaotic magnetic energy fields. This creates stress in the body.

Stress is always the antithesis to awareness and presence. This is one important reason why people do yoga and why they do various other preliminary practices - to release the stress and tension that builds up in the body.

Of course there are a myriad of techniques, methods and ways you can release stress. One of the most important is getting outside and putting your feet on the ground.

This will greatly help in dissipating the buildup of electro-magnetic energy. This energy gets trapped in the body making the mind spin faster. Any stress is going to make the mind think more.

I highly encourage that you combine this 10 minute practice with being on the earth. You should be doing that for natural health purposes anyway, at least once a day.

Participant 7: Actually I became quite amused with myself

Kevin: That's good, amusement is always good.

Participant 7: *Anyhow, I would just lead myself on a merry chase and I would have to pull myself back. I also used the breath, breathing up and down in that area but still I was a kite and had to pull back.*

Kevin: That is normal and that's why it takes practice because all of us have developed these deep unconscious grooves in our being. It is going to take time to create new grooves and to re-pattern the old ones. Sometimes the old ones can be very stubborn to change. It can take a lot of intentional work to re-shift those patterns – that's fine.

Participant 8: *When you said to do the exercise, I focused on my belly and I felt incredible squeezing and tightness. It was very tight like I was being squeezed and my sudden response to that was I need to breath deeper into this and I started to really breath deeper into it.*

It opened and unlocked and then my mind came into it and started commenting on what was going on. Then the next thing that happened was that I suddenly thought I am a little bored with this but I will keep on doing it.

It was like I split my attention and my awareness and I was breathing into this and doing that but at the same time I took part of my attention up to my third eye. I was in this really nice purple place up there, enjoying myself – so there were a lot of things going on.

Kevin: Well the first really interesting thing about what you were saying, and many people may notice this, is that this energy center in the abdominal region, as in the heart and the brain, is constricted and tight.

When you start to bring a focus to it, awareness to it, it is quite normal that you notice how tight it is. It's like geez I didn't realize that I was holding this much tension – it feels like its being strangled there. The sense of being strangled, the sense of tension, tightness, constriction, is normal.

This really validates what I was saying earlier about the energy – if this vital energy center of the body is tight and constricted, it pushes the energy up to the brain. When it pushes the energy up to the brain it is going to spin the mind. This makes it next to impossible to be Present.

Energy has to go somewhere. Until you develop mastery in the body and can be really present, you cannot stay focused in the mind and remain present as well.

You may go into transcendence which relates to the energy in parts the brain, but this does not help to develop Presence. When you were noticing the purples you were focused in the brain. A lot of people who meditate experience these colors in their inner vision. This is not what you are looking to cultivate.

If it's there that's fine. I am not saying that there is anything wrong with it, but you have to remember what you are really wanting to learn is how to ground the focus of your mind in the Hara region of the body. Otherwise, you are always at the mercy of a chaotic mind.

What is this course about? It's about Mastery. It's about mastering your human experience through the Sacred Trinity of Body, Mind and Heart-Spirit, which relate to your spiritual journey.

These are the beginning steps of mastery. You have to be responsible for how your energy system works and if it is not working well, you have to be responsible for that too.

You would think that would just be a normal human area of responsibility, but we are not usually taught this as children or in school.

We are taught to be responsible for our check books, our finances, and our relationships. What about being responsible for the energy that makes up our human life experience?

Participant 6: *For me it was really hard to focus in that area. I could feel tightness and feeling a spaghetti rope everywhere and a lot of anxiety. There was something that wanted to release and just let go and after that there was nothing*

Kevin: Again this brings up some great points. As you do these practices you will notice that the tension that is there is usually in the form of various emotional energies. The Taoist system relates the kidneys to this area and the kidneys relate to the water energy system which relates to fear.

When you have fear your internal energy freezes just like what happens to water when it freezes. It becomes rigid which is felt in the body as tension. Fear, anxiety and tension do reside in this area of the body.

One part of human mastery is the ability to consciously get blocked emotional energy to flow again. At times this can be quite uncomfortable and can very difficult because in doing so, there may be a tremendous amount of unconscious emotional energy to be experienced and processed.

I am not saying or even implying that by doing these practices that you are going to always have blissful, joyful experiences.

You will have a roller coaster ride. At times you will be up and you will think hey this is great and at other times you will feel lousy. You will feel bored, anxious and so on. You will feel a whole range of emotions.

Part of Mastery is learning to be with those difficult emotions. Becoming a Divine Human is learning to be able to be with difficult and uncomfortable feelings and uncomfortable energies. This is a very important part of the journey actually.

Participant 9: Unfortunately I was kind of in and out so I missed the part where you said to focus – but nothing really was going on and when you said come back I saw a really small picture in a black frame in my gut...

Kevin: Again what we have been talking about through this session is cultivating focus. For many people this is really new - unless you have intentionally practiced something similar for a long time.

Even those of you who have been on the spiritual path for a while may be much more used to focusing in the third eye and the heart rather than the hara. These are the upper chakras and energy centers, whereas really we have to start in the basement.

You have got to clean up the basement first which is the abdominal sexual area. These are the lower chakras and energy centers.

I would highly encourage you even if you have been on a certain path for a while, to clean up the trash in the basement. Start from there.

I know from personal experience that you have to ground the energy and you can't ground the energy if that part of your being has not been dealt with and mastered to a significant degree.

Even though you may have heard in the past to first focus on the third eye and the crown, dealing with the hara is really the first step. Focusing on the third eye and crown is really saying forget about the body. Well, we are reversing that process here.

I think this was a great session. We covered a lot of key points for this first week of practice in the Awakened Heart Mastery Course.

I thank each one of you for your participation and as always I encourage you to remember to A.C.T. It is all about Awareness, Cultivation and Transformation. It is with love and blessings that I bid you farewell in this moment, until next week.

APPENDIX FOUR

Personal Spiritual Mentoring
Program With Kevin Hunter

- A monthly program via phone, webcam or in person.
- Minimum time commitment 6 months after an initial interview.
- Save years of ineffective struggle on your spiritual path.
- Learn to balance and evolve holistically in Body, Mind and Heart-Spirit.
- Awaken and Experience Authentic Love, Peace and Happiness.

A rare opportunity for Direct Spiritual Guidance

For those Souls with a burning intention and desire to Awaken their Heart and to make the most out of their human spiritual journey, direct guidance and facilitation with Kevin is available to limited number of people.

The Spiritual Journey is full of subtle intricacy and complexity. There is a tremendous amount of inner and outer work to be done in order for an individual to successfully align the Sacred Trinity of Body, Mind and Heart-Spirit.

Each of these dimensions needs to be properly integrated in order for an individual's personal awakening and transformation to occur, in the most direct and efficient manner possible.

Throughout mankind's history most spiritual seekers worked with and received personal guidance from an Enlightened Teacher within the context of a small group of fellow seekers.

This allowed the Teacher to know each person's ego patterns and to know where, when and how to apply assistance so that the individual could Awaken beyond their personal limitations and boundaries.

It is very difficult and an almost impossible task, for an individual to Awaken on their own beyond the self-imposed energetic contractions and limitations of the ego.

Each individual has very subtle energetic, emotional, mental belief patterns that keep them asleep and unaware of the Truth of Reality.

Awakening is a real process that involves great transformation in order for it to be authentic. It is not about mental hopes and wishes for freedom and happiness. The Spiritual Teacher is your best friend, guide and a facilitator for you to actualize greater truth and freedom in this lifetime.

The Spiritual Mentoring Program

1. Addresses the Body, Mind and Heart-Spirit utilizing the Sacred Trinity Approach
   - Regular Study Material for the Mind
   - Diet, Exercise, Supplements
   - Heart Based Practices
   - Meditation Guidance

2. What is included:

    -   Monthly Phone Mentoring – 1 hour per month.
    -   Email support and follow up.
    -   Personal assignments and practices that lead to greater awakening and transformation.
    -   Online 16 Week Awakened Heart Mastery Course.
    -   Energetic Empowerment. This naturally takes place via the mentoring phone calls and emails as you will be in Kevin's personal focus and consideration well beyond the time spent in personal conversation.

3. Screening Process:

    -   Everyone who applies will be screened to insure that the person is willing to make the commitment that is required to participate in this program. If accepted, an agreement of practice will be signed.

        The initial interview will be with Kevin so that he can determine the sincerity and appropriateness of providing spiritual guidance to the individual who is applying.

4. Program Cost:

    -   $250 monthly with a 6 month to 1 year agreement.

Due to Kevin's overall responsibilities and time commitments he is only able to directly facilitate a limited number of people at any time. If and when a slot becomes available, you will be notified promptly.

APPENDIX FIVE

Spiritual Presence Empowerment
With Kevin Hunter

- Awaken Beyond the Ego

- Directly Experience Presence

- Ignite Your Spiritual Transformation

This is a 40 minute Direct Awakening Experience with Kevin either in person or via webcam.

It has always been understood that the quickest way to Awaken is through the Empowerment of someone who is already in the Awakened State you want to experience.

It is very difficult for any human being to go from a state of sleep or non-awareness, identified with their personality ego self, to a state of Pure Awareness.

Pure Awareness is free from any of the limitations that most people normally experience in relation to their physical body, emotions and thought patterns.

Normally people are trapped by their ego life patterns that obscure the direct experience of Presence. When a person is able to directly connect with "Presence" in the present moment, a vast inner space opens within them.

Where there was once a sense of limitation and unhappiness, there is now the space for innate joy, love and freedom to emerge.

Many spiritual traditions refer to this as your natural state of Being. The Spiritual Teacher, who is anchored in Presence, can facilitate an inner Awakening that reveals what you have always been – the Eternal Radiant Self.

Until an individual awakens to the direct experience of Presence their spiritual journey of inner transformation has not truly begun.

THE ENERGETIC PHYSICS OF SPIRITUAL AWAKENING

A significant role that the Teacher plays is that of Energetic Transformer. The Teacher having cleared and released many obstacles and blockage within their own energetic system becomes a conduit and channel for the subtle life force energy of Consciousness.

This is referred to as Presence. The more present the Teacher the greater the flow of life force and the greater potential transformation that an individual can experience.

When the individual surrenders their inner resistance there is an opening within that allows for Enlightening Presence, Energy and Awareness to enter.

It is this energy of Consciousness along with the individual's intention and focus that brings about a direct and efficient Awakening. Thus the Spiritual Teacher is an energy source of Enlightening Presence.

Spiritual Presence Empowerment

This Presence allows an individual to expand their awareness and to gain insight into themselves. In this way they can see and discover what is blocking Presence in each moment from manifesting directly, from within.

The whole point of engaging in the Spiritual Presence Empowerment with Kevin is to spark this process of Awakening within you.

Spiritual awakening is about creating your life in such a way that you can live with joy and happiness. The Spiritual Teacher is there to facilitate this intention.

What to expect in this Empowerment Session with Kevin

During this session Kevin will personally guide you into Presence via a number of methods depending on the individual and what is required to facilitate their Awakening to Presence.

This may include any of the following plus additional methods not listed here.

1. Guided Breath
2. Question and Response
3. Silence
4. Physical Movement
5. Direct Open Heart, Open Eye Contact and Transmission

Kevin will directly feel into your energy field and your inner structures of tension and resistance and artfully guide you to release what is obstructing you from experiencing Presence in the moment.

The Awakened Heart Path

Kevin focuses his own energetic Presence into the energy field of the person while the session is taking place. This energy usually lies beyond what can be directly perceived by an individual. However, it creates a positive shift in their vibrational field that assists in Awakening Presence and the effect of this energy continues well beyond the allocated time of the session.

Session Cost $125

APPENDIX SIX

Awakened Heart Vision

To create a collective community
to evolve the Spiritual Heart.

For humanity, 2012 and beyond is a new stage of spiritual development and cultivation of the Spiritual Heart, both within each individual Soul and for humanity as a whole.

It is about Spiritual Awakening that includes Body, Mind and Heart-Spirit. This is a radical departure from many of the Ancient Spiritual Teachings and the methods and techniques developed in the past, regarding spiritual transformation.

The Awakened Heart Path is centered on staying Present and Aware of the Body and its relationships. It is about bringing the energy of the Divine in and through the Heart and Circulating that energy of Loving Presence.

To facilitate this next stage of Spiritual Heart Awakening for a greater number of people, it is important to create a spiritual community that can act as a blueprint for other groups and cultures.

For those of you who resonate with the Awakened Heart Path and would like to unfold your life based on the principles and wisdom that this path provides, an intentional spiritual community such as this one, may be of interest to you.

The Awakened Heart Path

Here are some of the Key Principles of this Community

1. Developing insight and wisdom about the current stage of human evolution and how you can participate and be in alignment with it.

2. Having the intention to unfold the spiritual journey and being willing to take responsibility for your human life. That only you can enlighten yourself, only you can save yourself, only you can free yourself. This is not an external Savior or Guru path that will do it for you.

3. Progressive Growth and Transformation through Conscious Living and making Conscious Choices in which one gradually addresses and changes one's limiting patterns, behaviors, beliefs and actions.

4. The creation of a daily spiritual practice that helps to deepen inner spiritual awareness and connection to the body as well as the conscious development of the spiritual life force energy of the body.

5. The use of ancient wisdom and traditional methods along with cutting edge technology and other techniques and approaches that foster overall balanced growth physically, mentally, emotionally and spiritually.

6. The creation of the Awakened Heart Sanctuary. This will allow for longer meditation retreats to be offered as well as other types of programming to take place.

If any of the above interests you I encourage you to join the Awakened Heart Community Forum. Also if you have any skills, time or resources that you would like to contribute please contact me.

About the Author

From an early age, Kevin was aware of very sourceful states of Consciousness. When he was 5, he recalls walking with his Grandfather in an orange grove in Florida and being aware of a very blissful energy above the top of his head. It was a feeling of complete delight and freedom.

Gradually, however, this sense of innate happiness began to disappear and Kevin became painfully aware of being contained and confined, within and by, his body and mind. Over his early teenage years, Kevin found himself in a state of distress due to a feeling of deep inner unhappiness.

All through those early years, Kevin deeply questioned the meaning and purpose of his life. Then one afternoon, at the age of 18, Kevin had a spontaneous Awakening and direct knowledge of himself as Consciousness.

This profound experience inspired him to more fully comprehend this direct knowing of Consciousness so that it could ultimately be shared with other beings that were not yet Awakened to the greater Reality of life.

He began an in-depth study of the world's religions spanning Christianity, Buddhism, Sufism, Hinduism, Tibetan Buddhism, Shamanism, and Taoism, along with more modern approaches such as Trans-personal Psychology. At the same time, he began to practice yoga and the Zen meditation "zazen".

He has thoroughly studied physical purification, rejuvenation, emotional healing and clearing, as well as the development and integration of the human psyche. Over the years, Kevin has worked intensively to unravel the mysteries of human spiritual transformation within himself and progressively, within other souls.

Kevin has personally found that it is critical to develop in a holistic and balanced way by cultivating all our dimensions. He refers to these as "The Sacred Trinity", commonly known as body, mind and spirit.

This has led him to create and develop a concise, innovative approach to unraveling the deeper dimensions of the Spiritual Heart in relation to the spiritual journey of inner transformation.

Based on his direct experience, research, and contemplation of more than 25 years, Kevin has created, refined and evolved the Awakened Heart Path.